MANITOBA
BOOK OF
Everything

Everything you wanted to know about
Manitoba and were going to ask anyway

Christine Hanlon, Barbara Edie and Doreen Pendgracs

W9-CYS-647

MACINTYRE PURCELL PUBLISHING INC.

MacIntyre Purcell Publishing Inc.
232 Lincoln St., Suite D
PO Box 1142
Lunenburg, Nova Scotia
B0J 2C0
(902) 640-3350
www.bookofeverything.com
info@bookofeverything.com

Cover photo courtesy: Doug Dealey
istockphoto: page 6, 8, 22, 36, 44, 60, 74, 88, 112, 132, 158, 176 and 196

Printed and bound in Canada.

Library and Archives Canada Cataloguing in Publication
Hanlon, Christine
Manitoba Book of Everything: everything you wanted to know about
Manitoba and were going to ask anyway / Christine Hanlon, Barbara
Edie and Doreen Pendgracs.
ISBN 978-0-9784784-5-2
1. Manitoba. 2. Manitoba--Miscellanea. I. Edie, Barbara
II. Pendgracs, Doreen III. Title.

FC3361.6.H36 2008   971.27
C2008-903297-7

Introduction

No book could possibly cover everything about Manitoba, but we hope this collection of facts, lists, anecdotes and profiles captures the spirit of the Keystone Province. It's a land of harsh and quiet beauty, unforgiving at times, yet as anyone who has set foot in the province can attest, Manitoba is also a colourful, inviting and diverse place.

Whether you're a visitor to our beloved province, or have grown up eating perogies and swatting mosquitoes like this book's three writers, we're sure you'll uncover a few surprises within these pages. You'll also have plenty of opportunity to smile at the familiar — the Royal Winnipeg Ballet, icy winters and Margaret Laurence included — for which we are best known. I could go on and on about the late Winnipeg Jets, the Great Flood, Louis Riel and The Guess Who, but I'd still only be scratching the surface. If you really want to learn about Manitoba's illustrious writers, crazy lingo and notorious criminals, you'll just have to crack open this little book.

Barbara Edie tackled the "Slang," "Place Names," "Natural World" and "Weather" chapters, while Doreen Pendgracs wrote the "Culture" and "First Nations" entries, and I handled the rest. The project wouldn't have been possible without the creative conception of John MacIntyre at MacIntyre Purcell Publishing, as well as the work of Kelly Inglis. Thanks also to our editor, Tim Lehnert, whose patience, sense of humour and words of wisdom guided us along our journey.

We would also like to thank all those Manitobans who took the time to give us a personal glimpse of our province in the form of Take 5 lists. The temperature may drop to forty below at Winnipeg's Portage and Main, but your insightful contributions truly represent the warm heart of Manitoba!

> — Christine Hanlon, for everyone who worked to
> bring you the *Manitoba Book of Everything*

Table of Contents

Moody Manitoba Morning

"Moody Manitoba Morning" was written and recorded by Rick Neufeld, and later re-recorded by the Bells in 1969. It became the theme song for Manitoba's Centennial in 1970. Credit goes to Cancon Music Publishing (SOCAN) for their permission to reprint these fine lyrics.

It's a moody Manitoba morning
Nothing's really happening, it never does
Just got up and waited for the mailman
To bring me a letter that never was
I'm not sad or happy, just living day by day

It's a moody Manitoba morning
I like it that way
It's a long and kind of gentle
Lazy prairie town afternoon
The sky is high
I can fell the grass growing
From yesterday's rain
Sun's a glowing and so am I
Read the afternoon paper
To see where the world was at

It's a long and kind of gentle lazy day
I like it like that
It's a quiet, welcome, lively
Sort of leisurely past the evening
It's after nine
Go slowly walking up and down
The main street with a special girl
Things are fine

Now it's time to go home
Tomorrow's another day
Another moody Manitoba morning
And we like it that way
Another moody Manitoba morning
(come on now)

Moody Manitoba morning (5x)
And we like it that way

Manitoba:

A Timeline

10,000-13,000 years before present: Nomadic hunters enter Manitoba from the southwest. Developing grasslands in the south provide abundant hunting territory while Lake Agassiz covers much of the province's remaining land.

4,000-5,000 years before present: Hunters populate the Canadian Shield in the eastern and northern part of the province after Glacial Lake Agassiz recedes, leaving behind lakes Winnipeg and Manitoba.

1610: Henry Hudson sails the *Discovery* into Hudson Bay.

1612: First Europeans set foot in Manitoba when Thomas Button winters two ships at Port Nelson, near the mouths of the Nelson and Hayes Rivers.

1619: Danish explorer Jens Munck enters Churchill Harbour in the *Unicorn* and builds a temporary house on shore.

1668: In search of new sources of fur, Radisson and Groseilliers sail for Hudson Bay in the *Nonsuch*.

1670: England's King Charles II creates Rupert's Land and grants a charter to the Hudson's Bay Company (HBC).

1684: York Factory is founded as the HBC's main trading post on the Hudson Bay Coast.

1691: HBC employee Henry Kelsey explores Northern Manitoba from Hudson Bay to the Saskatchewan River, near The Pas. He is the first European to see and describe the buffalo.

1738: Quebec-born explorer Pierre Gaultier de Varennes, Sieur de la Vérendrye, builds Fort Rouge at the forks of the Red and Assiniboine Rivers.

1754: Anthony Henday sets out to explore the interior of the province in an expedition funded by the HBC in response to concerns that La Vérendrye is funneling the fur trade to his forts.

1731-1771: The British build Fort Prince of Wales at the mouth of the Churchill River.

1779: The North West Fur Company is established in Montreal.

1783: After Fort Prince of Wales is temporarily captured and then badly damaged by the French in 1782, the HBC constructs Fort Churchill. The fort is in continuous use by the company until 1933.

1793: Cuthbert Grant Senior founds a trading post for the North West Company on the Assiniboine River three miles above the Souris River mouth. Meanwhile, the HBC penetrates as far south as the Red and Assiniboine Rivers, founding Brandon House on the Assiniboine three miles above the North West Company's post.

1809: The North West Company builds Fort Gibraltar at the forks of the Red and Assiniboine Rivers.

1811: Lord Selkirk purchases Assiniboia from the HBC and establishes an agricultural settlement. Hundreds of people from England, Scotland and Ireland begin settling in the Red River Valley area.

1814: Miles Macdonnell issues the "Pemmican Proclamation," which prohibits the export of food from the Selkirk Settlement.

1816: Governor Robert Semple and 19 colonists are killed in a battle with the Métis at Seven Oaks during a dispute over changing lifestyles along the Red River.

1821: The HBC and the North West Company amalgamate.

1822: Fort Gibraltar is renamed Fort Garry, in honour of Nicholas Garry, the HBC deputy governor who supervised the amalgamation.

1826: The greatest recorded flood in the history of Manitoba almost destroys the Selkirk settlement.

1829: Two Métis sisters, Angelique and Marguerite Nolan, begin teaching at the first school for girls in western Canada.

1834: The HBC repurchases Assiniboia from the Selkirk estate.

1846: British troops are stationed in the colony.

1847: The results of Métis trader Pierre Sayer's trial for illegally trafficking in furs are ambiguous, and ultimately allow for free trade in furs, challenging the HBC's monopoly.

1859: The *Anson Northup* becomes the first steamboat on the Red River.

Lord Selkirk and the Red River Colony

Thomas Douglas, the Fifth Earl of Selkirk, was the very definition of tenacity. Born in Scotland in 1771 to an aristocratic family, he was never expected to inherit his family's title or money. But by 1799, after the death of his older brothers, he had both.

Philanthropic in nature, Selkirk used his newfound wealth to purchase land and settle poor Scottish farmers in Ireland, Prince Edward Island, Upper Canada and, later, at Red River, a part of Rupert's Land. It was while visiting the Scottish Highlands during his law school days that he first became concerned for the plight of "crofters" or landless peasants.

When the British government refused to grant him lands to continue his resettlement plans (because Rupert's Land belonged to the Hudson's Bay Company) Selkirk started purchasing shares in the corporation.

In 1808, Selkirk and his family effectively gained control of the HBC. Three years later, the company granted him 116,000 square miles to found an agricultural settlement at Red River. Led by Governor Miles Macdonnell, the first party of 128 settlers arrived at the forks of the Red and Assiniboine Rivers in 1812.

But success would prove elusive. From the start, the settlement was opposed by the North West Company (NWC) and its Métis traders who, not incorrectly, saw the initiative as an attempt to disrupt their trade in fur. Arriving just before winter, the settlers missed the planting season and had to depend on the very Métis they were alienating. In 1884, Macdonnell responded to the endemic shortage of food by issuing the Pemmican Proclamation forbidding the export of food from the entire area. The Métis, who survived by selling

1869: Louis Riel and his men seize Fort Garry and set up a provisional government.

pemmican (a portable mixture of dried ground meat and fat) to NWC traders, retaliated by burning the settlement to the ground.

In response, Selkirk sent more settlers to Red River and appointed Robert Semple as governor. Reports that he planned to send 1,000 families to the region within 10 years only heightened tensions with the Métis. The situation exploded in 1816 at the Battle of Seven Oaks during which the Métis and their NWC partners killed Semple and nineteen of his men.

When Selkirk heard that the NWC had imprisoned several settlers at Fort William (now part of the Ontario city of Thunder Bay) he led a private army to occupy the fort and impound all the furs. He also arrested and charged several NWC officials with the deaths of the men at Seven Oaks. Selkirk's vigilante justice went awry, however, when the nine men drowned on the way to be tried in Montreal.

A warrant was issued for his arrest, but Selkirk refused to comply. Instead, he made a visit to Red River in 1817 and then took a circuitous route through the United States before finally arriving in Montreal to address the charges. Unable to clear his name, he returned to Britain in late 1818. By that time, he was already suffering from consumption. He died in Pau, France in 1820.

Selkirk's legacy did not die with him. Eventually, the Red River Settlement became the basis of an agrarian population that would attract further newcomers to the region. And because of the conflict he engendered, the Métis consolidated their identity during this period, eventually playing an instrumental role in the creation of Manitoba.

Selkirk's impact is immortalized in the province through the city of Selkirk, the Winnipeg neighbourhood of Point Douglas, and the city's renowned Selkirk Avenue. A statue of Lord Selkirk is located at the east entrance of the Manitoba Legislative Building.

1870: As a result of the provisional government's initiatives, Manitoba joins Confederation. Winnipeg becomes the capital of the new "Postage Stamp" province (1/18 its current size) and of the Northwest Territories.

Take 5 MANITOBA MUSEUM'S FIVE
SIGNIFICANT ARTIFACTS

The Manitoba Museum, with its Planetarium and Science Centre, is the largest heritage attraction in the province. The museum combines natural and social history themes, and explores the history and environment of the entire province. Sharon Reilly, Curator of Social History, selected five artifacts from the Museum's Parklands/Mixed-Woods Gallery that are used to interpret the history of Manitoba immigration and settlement, and the province's social, political, and economic life.

1. **Hand-knotted Caucasian Carpet, pre-1870.** German-speaking Russian Mennonite immigrants to Manitoba gave this carpet to Canadian immigration agent Wilhelm Hespeler in thanks for facilitating their migration to Canada. Government officials, transportation agents and others played a role in the migration of thousands of newcomers to western Canada following Confederation. Traveling in Russia in 1871, Hespeler met Mennonites who wished to leave to find religious freedom, and he helped hundreds of these people to immigrate to Manitoba.

2. **The Association of United Ukrainian Canadians (AUUC) Banner, early 20th century.** This hand painted, silk banner is from the AUUC at the Ukrainian Labour Temple in north-end Winnipeg. The AUUC was one of many mutual aid societies that flourished in early Manitoba. With their secret rituals and elaborate regalia, these organizations served as the building blocks of a new society. They provided essential sick benefits and burial assistance to their members, and helped to preserve social and cultural traditions.

1871: The first session of the first Manitoba Legislature opens. The first public school opens in Winnipeg, and the first telegram is sent from Manitoba.

3. **Birthing Mat, c.1921.** This artifact was owned by a midwife in rural Manitoba and conjures up a vivid image of childbirth in isolated communities in early Manitoba. Used as an absorbent bed covering during childbirth, the mat was made from a stack of newspaper (in this case, the *Free Press Prairie Farmer*, dated June 22 and 29, 1921) encased within a hand-sewn cotton and cheesecloth cover. The fabric has been repaired all over, indicating that it was washed and re-used regularly.

4. **Sugar Beet Knife, c. 1942.** A Japanese-Canadian used this tool on a Manitoba farm during the Second World War. After Japan attacked Pearl Harbor in 1941, the Canadian government seized properties owned by Japanese-Canadians on the west coast and interned most families at isolated work camps in British Columbia. Some were sent to prairie sugar beet farms. Forced to live in appalling conditions, they struggled just to survive. In 1988, the Canadian government apologized for this injustice and announced a redress settlement.

5. **Mary Maxim "Eagle" Sweater c. 1946-48.** This sweater was hand-knit using an early pattern produced by Mary Maxim Limited in Sifton, Manitoba. The first woolen mills here were opened in the 1930s, and for many years wool-related industries brought prosperity to the town. The most successful of these was Mary Maxim. In 1954, the growing company moved to nearby Dauphin, and then opened facilities in Paris, Ontario and another in Port Huron, Michigan. The Dauphin office was closed in 1958.

The Golden Boy

On November 1, 1919, a gilded five-ton lad took his place atop the dome of the Manitoba Legislature, more than 76 m above the ground. It had been a long journey.

The 5.25-metre-tall figure was sculpted by Charles Gardet in Paris, France and cast in bronze in 1918 at the nearby Barbidienne foundry. Although the foundry was bombed during the First World War, the boy escaped unscathed and was whisked away to a wheat freighter. The Golden Boy then languished as the French government commandeered the ship to transport troops.

Packed in straw within the cargo hold, the golden statue became ballast as the ship continued its war service. Throughout the war, the boy was transported back and forth through the submarine infested waters of the Atlantic, the North Sea and the Mediterranean. Eventually the war ended and the figure disembarked, as planned, at a pier in Halifax. Loaded onto a flat car, The Golden Boy headed for his ultimate destination, finally arriving in Winnipeg in August 1919.

Since then, the Golden Boy has become one of Manitoba's best known symbols. Embodying the spirit of enterprise and eternal youth, he raises a torch in his right hand as a call to all those who join in moving the province forward. In fact, his stance is that of a runner. Poised on his left foot, the Golden Boy faces north, the source of minerals, fish, forests, furs and hydro-electric power on which Manitoba's future is built. In his left arm, he holds a sheaf of wheat, symbolizing the province's important agricultural heritage.

The boy wasn't always golden; he developed his characteristic aspect in the 1940s thanks to a coat of paint, and in 1951 donned a shining suit of 23 karat gold. The torch was illuminated in 1970 as part of Manitoba's Centennial Celebrations. In February 2002, the Golden Boy was taken down from his perch for repairs and re-gilding. He resumed his position in Winnipeg's skyline on September 5, 2002 when he was rededicated by Queen Elizabeth II during her Golden Jubilee tour of Canada.

1872: First number of the *Manitoba Free Press* appears.

1874: The first Mennonites arrive in Manitoba from Russia. Meanwhile, in Winnipeg's first civic election, only white men of means are allowed to vote. Voters have to be male, at least 21 years of age, British subjects by birth or naturalization, and own property valued at $100 or more, or pay at least $20 per year in rent.

1875: The first Icelandic settlers arrive.

1876: The Northwest Territories Act is passed, separating it from Manitoba. The first wheat is shipped out of Manitoba. The Indian Act is implemented in western Canada, creating the reservation system.

1877: The University of Manitoba receives its Charter. The first railway locomotive arrives in St. Boniface, and the first telephone is installed in Winnipeg.

1882: Manitoba's first electric light appears on Main Street in Winnipeg.

1883: Manitoba adopts Standard time.

1885: Louis Riel is executed at Regina.

1889: The first Winnipeg Bonspiel is held. This bonspiel becomes the leading curling event in Canada until the Brier begins in 1927.

1890: The dual system of French Catholic and English Protestant schools is abolished.

1892: The first two Ukrainians reach Winnipeg. Meanwhile, the city sees its first electric street cars.

Take 5 PETER WARREN'S FIVE
MOST MEMORABLE INTERVIEWS

A member of the Canadian Broadcast Hall of Fame, investigative journalist Peter Warren was City Editor of the *Winnipeg Tribune* before jumping to radio where he hosted CJOB's "Action-Line" for 27 years. He then hosted the coast-to-coast program "Warren On The Weekend" for ten years on the Corus Radio Network from CKNW in Vancouver. He is now a freelance writer/broadcaster specializing in cold-case murder and wrongful-conviction cases. A life-long journalist, Warren has worked around the world, in print and over the airwaves.

1. **Joe Borowski versus Dr. Henry Morgentaler, re abortion.** Both were in-studio, this was the ONLY program where I had to separate guests before they engaged in a physical free-for-all. I believe the Manitoba cabinet minister would have felled the doctor with one punch if I had allowed them to engage in fisticuffs.

2. **Prime Minister Pierre-Elliot Trudeau.** He made the comment: "Warren is worse than Question Period," after the program. He'd given me a withering look and a dry "none of your business" when I asked whether he and then-wife Margaret would soon be receiving a Baby-Bonus cheque.

3. **Four escaped convicts gave themselves up on-the-air at different times.** It amused me that police surrounding the radio station were unable to act until each of them had been given time to tell his story.

4. **Prime Minister John Turner.** Incredibly, when I asked him about the Canadian Wheat Board monopoly, he pulled "flash cards" from the top pocket of his jacket and just read verbatim what flacks had written for him under "Agriculture."

5. **A child-education expert from Chicago (name not recalled) was in studio to discuss the growing problem of kids acting up.** Aged (I would guess) over 65, a nice, grey-haired "little old lady," she floored me when she replied to one question: "Look, Mr. Warren, kids say 'f@ck, p!ss and sh!t' so get used to it." I was so dumb-founded, I neglected to hit the "DELETE" button. And, more to the point, there was not one listener complaint.

1897: The Laurier-Greenway settlement resolves the Manitoba Schools Question by guaranteeing French education in schools with a minimum of 10 French-speaking pupils and re-establishing a Catholic school board, but without government funding. The guarantee is removed in 1916.

1906: The Timothy Eaton Company opens a department store in Winnipeg.

1907: The telephone system is purchased by the Manitoba government.

1910: The first boat passes through the St. Andrew's Lock.

1912: A final boundary change, north to 60°, renders Manitoba its current size.

1916: Manitoba introduces prohibition under the Manitoba Temperance Act. Women obtain the right to vote in Manitoba provincial elections.

1918: The Spanish influenza reaches epidemic proportions. Public meetings are banned in Manitoba.

1919: The Winnipeg General Strike brings work to a standstill for 40 days. Sympathy strikes occur in Brandon and other Canadian cities. The Greater Winnipeg Aqueduct is completed, bringing water to Winnipeg from Shoal Lake. The Golden Boy is placed on the dome of the new Legislative Building.

1923: Prohibition ends and the Liquor Control Commission is enacted.

1950: Major flooding occurs in southern Manitoba.

1952: Women are permitted to sit on juries in Manitoba courts. Manitoba Aboriginals are given the right to vote provincially.

1956: Stephen Juba becomes the first non-Anglo-Saxon mayor of Winnipeg.

1966: The Greater Winnipeg Floodway (Duff's Ditch) is officially opened.

1967: Winnipeg hosts the Pan American Games. The University of Winnipeg and Brandon University are chartered.

1970: Manitoba celebrates its centennial. Folklorama is part of the centenary activities and goes on to become a highly popular yearly festival celebrating Manitoba's ethnic and cultural communities.

1972: Unicity is formed, making Winnipeg the first large Canadian city to have its entire metropolitan area governed by a single municipal administration.

1979: Former Manitoba Premier Edward Schreyer becomes Canada's 22nd Governor General.

1980: The *Winnipeg Tribune* folds after 90 years of publication.

1985: The Supreme Court of Canada renders Manitoba's "English-only" laws invalid.

1990: NDP MLA Elijah Harper kills the Meech Lake Accord by voting against provincial approval.

1993: Métis leader Yvon Dumont is named Lieutenant-Governor of Manitoba, 108 years after the death of Louis Riel.

1996: The NHL Winnipeg Jets, who had debuted in 1972 as a member of the World Hockey Association, are moved to Phoenix, Arizona.

1997: The Red River overflows its banks in the "Flood of the Century" and 25,000 are forced to evacuate their homes.

1999: The Pan American Games are held in Winnipeg for the second time.

2003: Winnipeg media mogul and philanthropist Israel Asper passes away.

2006: Winnipeg speed skater Cindy Klassen becomes the first Canadian to win five medals in one Olympic Games.

2008: Manitoba loses out to Saskatchewan on the bid to host the 2010 Junior World Hockey Championship.

Manitoba Essentials

Location: Situated in the very centre of Canada, Manitoba is bounded by Saskatchewan to the west and Ontario to the east. Nunavut Territory lies to the north, and the US states of North Dakota and Minnesota are across the southern border.

Origin of the Name: From words in both Cree and Ojibway that refer to the straits formed by the Lake Manitoba Narrows. The waves washing over the limestone rocks sound like the Great Spirit "Manitou."

License Plate: Slogan changed to "Friendly Manitoba" from "100,000 Lakes" in 1976. The lake scene with bison graphic was added in 1997.

Motto: Gloriosus et Liber, "Glorious and Free"

Nicknames: The Keystone Province. Because of its position in the middle of Canada, Manitoba holds the country together like the keystone in an arch. Manitoba is also known as the Gateway to the West.

Coat of Arms: In 1905, King Edward VII granted Manitoba a coat of arms consisting of a shield with a bison and a cross. The original design was augmented in 1992 by then Canadian Governor General Ramon Hnatyshyn. A gold helmet now lies above the shield, and on top of that is a beaver holding Manitoba's provincial flower (the prairie crocus). A crown caps the beaver, and a unicorn and a horse support the left and right sides. Other elements include the wheel of a Red River cart, and Aboriginal bead and bone decorations. Manitoba's diverse landscape is represented by a base of wheat, crocuses, pine and water, and is underlined by a banner bearing the provincial motto.

Provincial Flag: Manitoba's official flag is the Red Ensign bearing the provincial coat of arms. Given royal approval by Her Majesty Queen Elizabeth II in October 1965, the flag was officially proclaimed by the Manitoba Legislative Assembly on May 12, 1966.

Tartan: Registered in Scotland as the official tartan, the Manitoba Tartan received royal assent in 1962. Each colour has its own significance: dark red squares refer to Manitoba's natural resources; azure blue lines represent Lord Selkirk, founder of the Red River Settlement (Winnipeg); dark green lines highlight the province's many ethnic groups; and golden lines signify grain and other agricultural products.

Provincial Bird: Chosen to represent Manitoba by naturalists and school groups, the Great Gray Owl was officially adopted as the provincial bird on July 16, 1987. The Great Gray, North America's largest owl, resides throughout Manitoba year-round, from the south-eastern corner of the province, west to Riding Mountain National Park and north to the tree line.

Provincial Flower: The prairie crocus (*anemone patens*) was officially adopted as the floral emblem of the province in 1906. One of the first plants to pierce through the winter snow, the delicate purple flower is known as the harbinger of spring.

Provincial Tree: The white spruce has been used extensively by traditional and modern cultures, and is a disease-resistant evergreen found throughout the province.

Provincial Animal: The bison once roamed the Manitoba grasslands in the thousands. This powerful animal continues to have spiritual significance for the province's Aboriginal peoples.

Entry into Confederation: 1870

Time Zone: Central Standard Time

Area Code: 204

Postal Code Span: All postal codes in Manitoba start with the letter "R".

Statutory Holidays: On September 25, 2007, the Manitoba government announced the creation of a new statutory holiday, Louis Riel Day, to be held every third Monday in February. Other statutory holidays are New Year's Day, Good Friday, Victoria Day, Canada Day, Civic Holiday (the first Monday in August), Labour Day, Remembrance Day, Thanksgiving Day, Christmas Day and Boxing Day.

Capital City: Winnipeg

Largest City: Winnipeg; population 633,451. Winnipeg's census metropolitan area population is 712,700.

System of Measurement: Metric

Voting Age: 18

Drinking Age: 18

Take 5 HOLLY MCNALLY'S FIVE
ESSENTIAL READS BY MANITOBA AUTHORS

Holly McNally is co-owner of Winnipeg based McNally Robinson Booksellers, Canada's largest independent bookseller. McNally Robinson also has stores in Calgary, Saskatoon and Toronto.

1. **Laurence, Margaret.** *The Stone Angel.* Toronto: New Canadian Library, 1988. Margaret Laurence was born in Neepawa, Manitoba in 1926. She wrote five novels about the fictional town of Manawaka, a place patterned after her birthplace and its people. *The Stone Angel* is a classic, easily the most memorable and moving of the five.

2. **Shields, Carol.** *The Republic Of Love.* Toronto: Vintage Canada, 1994. Although *The Republic of Love* did not receive the acclaim of her signature novel *The Stone Diaries*, it is as good as anything the great author has written and a perfectly charming and revealing portrait of Winnipeg to boot. The novel is a valentine to the city.

3. **Boyens, Ingeborg, ed.** *Encyclopedia of Manitoba.* Winnipeg: Great Plains Publications, 2007. This weighty tome invigorates a sense of ourselves as Manitobans and by doing so defines our place in the world. Written, edited and published by Manitobans, it contains 2,000 entries and essays. This book makes one beam with pride (even if you are not included). There is much to be applauded here.

4. **Toews, Miriam.** *A Complicated Kindness.* Toronto: Vintage Canada, 2005. Winner of the Governor General's Award in 2004, this droll authentic novel captures with devastating accuracy life in a fundamentalist Mennonite town in rural Manitoba. We adore Nomi Nickel, the wry, rebellious sixteen-year-old protagonist whose refreshing narrative voice is as strong as any you will come upon. Humour and tragedy combine in a brilliant tour de force.

5. **MacDonald, Jake.** *The Houseboat Chronicles, Notes from a Life in Shield Country.* Toronto: McClelland & Stewart, 2004. Since Manitobans have been flocking to the Canadian Shield for decades, laying a moral if not legal claim to this glorious northern geography, *The Houseboat Chronicles* is an apt entry here. Jake MacDonald spent years working and exploring in Shield country. His is a "floating cottage" and his experience is not that of a summer sojourn in cottage country, but a personal and committed journey into its wild places. Beautiful writing evokes a beautiful place.

POPULATION

Total Population: 1,193,566 (2008)
Male: 49.7 percent
Female: 50.3 percent
Rural: 28 percent
Urban: 72 percent

POPULATION DENSITY (PEOPLE/KM^2)

Manitoba	2.1
Alberta	4.6
Ontario	12.6
Nova Scotia	17.8
Toronto	3,939
New York City	10,194

POPULATION IN PERSPECTIVE

Manitoba has more people per square kilometre than Saskatchewan, but only half the population density of Alberta. All three prairie provinces have approximately the same area. Manitoba is the fifth largest Canadian province in terms of population, and is sixth in area. That puts it virtually at the centre of everything! About two thirds of Manitoba residents are concentrated in the capital city of Winnipeg.

IMMIGRATION AND POPULATION CHANGE

In 2007, Manitoba's population increased by more than 13,000, fueled mainly by overseas immigration. Eleven thousand people from abroad moved to Manitoba in 2007, with Filipinos representing over a quarter of the total. The province is hoping to attract 20,000 immigrants from overseas annually within the next decade. Manitoba is also currently gaining modest numbers of Canadians from other provinces, after years of losing residents to other parts of Canada. Manitoba is expected to reach the 1.2 million mark in population in 2009.

YOU KNOW YOU'RE FROM

- You switch the thermostat from heat to A/C several times in one day.
- You can swat and kill a mosquito without even looking.
- Your eyes get moist upon seeing a Jets logo.
- You've had your car broken into, stolen, or know someone who has.
- You shake your head at those who claim -20C is the end of the world as we know it.
- Someone says, "Let's go to the beach!" — and you know there is only one — and it's Grand!
- Your local Dairy Queen is closed from September through May.
- You consider it a sport to drill through 36 inches of ice and sit by the hole all day hoping food will swim by.
- Thanks to the logo on your license plate, you can still be "Friendly" when you cut someone off.
- You know all four seasons: Almost winter, winter, still winter, and construction.
- All your favourite local bands make it big and move to Toronto.
- You can be an Easterner or a Westerner depending on your mood.
- You argue the merits of boiled versus fried perogies.
- You spend summer holidays at the cottage, not the cabin.
- Any day is a good day for a slurpee from Sev (Seven Eleven).
- You measure distance in hours.
- You carry jumper cables in your car and the whole family knows how to use them.
- You design your kid's Halloween costume to fit over a snowsuit.
- Driving is better in the winter because the potholes are filled with snow.
- You call jelly-filled donuts Jambusters.
- You've been to Sals (Salisbury House) for a "nip."
- You remember the dates of major blizzards and floods.
- You know about Sunday Cruise Night . . . and have participated.
- You have no problem driving an hour to a party.
- You've been to at least one wedding social.
- You know that the mosquito is really the provincial bird.

MANITOBA WHEN . . .

- You get to the airport a half hour before your flight, yet the place is so empty that you still get on the plane -- with ease.
- You know of at least 10 people who have moved to Calgary.
- You know that Flin Flon is an actual place and not a made up name.
- You know exactly what to do with a sandbag.
- You aren't surprised when the weather changes from +5C to -50C within a week.
- You notice that the highest elevation point within a 16 km radius is the snow disposal site.
- You're as likely to shout "Halloween apples" as "trick-or-treat."
- You leave the shovel, scraper, mitts, etc. in your car year round.
- You call it a "bar," not a "club."
- You know how to parallel park on a snowbank.
- You brag that at least it's a DRY cold.
- You start your car every hour when you can't plug it in.
- You don't use turn signals.
- You've used your ice scraper on the INSIDE of your car window.
- You've played sponge hockey.
- You have been to Gimli and know it is not just a character in Lord of the Rings.
- Every second car you see is either a Pontiac Sunfire or a Chevy Cavalier.
- You plan your outfit in the summer according to how bad the mosquitoes are going to be.
- You see a bison and instantly think of MTS (the phone company).
- You have never had to sell or otherwise dispose of an old bicycle because every one you've ever owned has been stolen.
- You can't wait for the temperature to turn really cold so the community centre can flood the outdoor rink.
- The houses on your street have their Christmas lights hanging throughout the year.
- You know "going to the LC" means buying a bottle at the Liquor Control Commission.

POPULATION BY AGE AND SEX (2007)

Age	Male	Female	Total
0-14	115,565	109,610	225,175
15-64	378,450	382,885	761,335
65+	69,255	92,630	161,885

Source: Statistics Canada.

MEDIAN AGE

Men	36.3
Women	38.5

LIFE EXPECTANCY

Men	Manitoba 76.4	Canada	77.4
Women	Manitoba 81.4	Canada	82.4

FERTILITY RATE

On average, women in Manitoba have 1.8 children, substantially higher than the national average of 1.5.

CRADLE TO GRAVE

Births (2007)	14,200
Deaths (2007)	10,355

Did you know...

that during WWI, soldier Harry Colebourne bought a black bear cub as a mascot for his regiment and named it "Winnipeg" after his home town? He later donated the cub to the London Zoo, and when British author A.A. Milne visited the zoo with his son Christopher Robin, the bear became the inspiration for the famous stories.

Take 5 TOP FIVE MOST POPULOUS CITIES

1. **Winnipeg** (633,451)
2. **Brandon** (41,511)
3. **Thompson** (13,446)
4. **Portage La Prairie** (12,728)
5. **Steinbach** (11,066)

ON A TYPICAL DAY IN MANITOBA . . .

- 39 children are born
- 28 people die
- 16 marriages take place
- 6 people divorce

Source: Statistics Canada.

MARRIAGE

- Number of marriages: 5,746
- Rate of marriage in Manitoba: 4.9 (per 1,000 population)
- Marriage rate in Nunavut, Canada's lowest: 2.3
- Marriage rate in Prince Edward Island, Canada's highest: 6.0
- National marriage rate: 4.7
- Average age of groom at first marriage: 29.1
- Average age of bride at first marriage: 26.9

Source: Statistics Canada.

D-I-V-O-R-C-E

- The divorce rate (per 100 marriages) in Manitoba: 30.2
- The divorce rate in Quebec, the highest: 49.7
- The divorce rate in Prince Edward Island, the lowest: 27.3
- The divorce rate nationally: 38.3

Source: Statistics Canada.

Take 5 TOP FIVE LANGUAGES SPOKEN

1. **English**
2. **German**
3. **French**
4. **Tagalog** (Pilipino, Filipino)
5. **Ukrainian**

FAMILY STRUCTURE

- Number of all families (married and common law, single parent): 312,805
- Percentage of families with children: 61.8 percent
- Percentage of families without children: 38.2 percent
- Single parent (male): 3.3 percent
- Single parent (female): 13.7 percent

Source: Statistics Canada.

RELIGIOUS AFFILIATION (PERCENT)

- Protestant: 42.4
- Catholic: 28.9
- Other Christian: 4
- Christian Orthodox: 1.4
- Jewish: 1.2
- Other religions: 2.3
- None: 18.4

Source: Statistics Canada.

LANGUAGE

- Manitoba residents who speak more than one language: 211,400
- English and French: 103,525
- English and a non-official language: 14,875
- French and a non-official language: 110
- English, French and a non-official language: 105

Source: Statistics Canada.

FULL-TIME STUDENTS ENROLLED (2006)

- Universities: 36,126
- Colleges (Provincial): 10,001
- Other colleges: 2,847
- Public schools: 186,668
- Private or independent schools: 14,329
- Home schooling: 1,167
- Band operated: 17,718

Source: Government of Manitoba.

HIGHER EDUCATION

Manitoba has four universities: the University of Manitoba, the University of Winnipeg, Brandon University and the Collège universitaire de St. Boniface (CUSB). All four offer internationally-recognized Bachelor's and Master's degrees, and the University of Manitoba confers Doctoral degrees.

Founded in 1877, the University of Manitoba is the oldest university in western Canada. With an enrolment of 20,000 full-time and 15,000 part-time students, the campus is sometimes playfully called Manitoba's third largest city. The institution boasts a stellar international reputation in areas such as AIDs research and engineering, and received almost $155 million in research funding in 2006/07. Manitoba's only French-language post-secondary institution, CUSB, is affiliated with the University of Manitoba.

The University of Winnipeg is located downtown and is primarily an undergraduate university with a strong emphasis on the social sciences. More than 6,000 students attend full-time, and 5,000 part-time. The school received its charter in 1967; it evolved from United College, which had been formed in 1938 from the union of Manitoba and Wesley Colleges.

Brandon University enrolls 3,200 full-time and part-time students, and is well-known for its music program. Its origins date to 1899 when it was founded as a Baptist institution.

Take 5 SAMI JO SMALL'S FIVE FAVOURITE
MANITOBA OUTDOOR SPORTS MEMORIES

Growing up on Winnipeg's outdoor rinks, Sami Jo Small honed the skills that would take her to the Olympics three times, twice as goalie for Canada's Gold Medal women's hockey team. After earning her chops in boys' minor hockey with the St. Vital Victorias and Winnipeg Warriors, she played on Stanford University's men's team while earning her mechanical engineering degree. She is currently training hard for the 2010 Olympics in Vancouver.

1. **Tobogganing in racing sleds down the courses at St. Vital Park**. I loved going down, but always hated having to walk back up the slide. We used to walk in our giant snowsuits over to the park from my house, as if we were on an expedition around the world.

2. **Skating on the outdoor rinks in St. Vital**, (Norberry, Windsor, Glenlee, Greendell, Glenwood and Dakota). After skating all day, I'd feel my eyelashes freezing shut. I knew it was time to go in to warm up when I could no longer feel my feet. I felt so free on the outdoor rinks, hearing the ice crackle beneath my skates and imagining my dreams play out on the ice.

3. **Running my loop around St. Vital Park**. Because summers were so hot, I'd run in shaded areas to avoid the glaring sun. Meanwhile, in winter, my friends and I used to hammer nails through our running shoes to get some traction on the icy roads. The sidewalks were seldom paved, so we'd run right down the tire tracks in the middle of the road.

4. **Playing street hockey with all the local boys in the neighborhood**. We'd race home from school so we could grab our sticks and start playing. I mostly played in net, and made most of my own equipment, including a goalie mask I fabricated out of chicken wire, cardboard and duct tape.

5. **Track and Field Meets at the University of Manitoba Stadium**. Many a sunburn happened at these all-day meets pitting competitors from all over the province against one another.

The provincial government is hoping to increase enrollment at its community colleges, the largest of which, Red River College, has just over 7,000 full-time students. Another 7,000 students are spread out between Assiniboine College, University College of the North (formerly Keewatin College) and École technique et professionnelle, part of CUSB.

HEALTH CARE PROFESSIONALS

Physicians	2,125
Dentists	610
Nurses	14,510
Pharmacists	1,152

NEWS OF THE DAY

The *Winnipeg Free Press* and *Winnipeg Sun* are daily papers sold across the province. The other dailies are the *Brandon Sun*, the *Portage la Prairie Daily Graphic* and the *Flin Flon Daily Reminder*. Several municipalities have their own weekly newspapers, and Canstar publishes five Winnipeg neighbourhood weeklies as well as *Uptown*, the city's weekly arts and entertainment guide. Many ethnic and language groups have their own papers, including the Francophone community's *La Liberté*.

Weblinks

Unforgettable Manitoba

www.travelmanitoba.com

The official gateway to all things Manitoban, this user-friendly website is jam packed with information, trivia and ideas for exploring.

Manitoba in Photos

www.manitobaphotos.com

This private collection is a visual showcase of Manitoba, from its landmarks to its quiet beauty, from its culture to its people.

Slang:

Autopac: Manitoba's public auto insurance system.

Back 40: The land or field (usually about 40 acres) at the back of a rural property, usually far from the home site or farmyard.

BDI: The acronym used by Winnipeggers for the Bridge Drive Inn, an ice cream stand at the foot of a pedestrian bridge, and a Winnipeg institution.

Booter: A boot full of water and/or mud after stepping into water (or muck) higher than your rubber boots.

Buffalo chips: Dried pieces of buffalo (or bison) dung.

Bush party: A party in the back woods or country fields, usually involving a bonfire, teenagers and far too much beer.

Confusion Corner: An intersection near Winnipeg's Osborne Village that any driver not from Manitoba would be hard pressed to navigate.

Dainties: Small dessert squares, slices and sweets usually prepared for community events, bridal showers or church gatherings.

Dugout: A pond or reservoir on a farm.

Fall supper: A prairie tradition, a community dinner in a rural area that is open to the public. Usually held in September or October, it is also known as a "Fowl Supper," as turkey or chicken is often served.

Farmer vision: Also known as "country cable," it is found in rural areas that receive only four broadcast channels: CBC, CTV, Global and Citi TV (formerly the A-channel).

Faspa: A Mennonite word for a late afternoon meal or light supper.

Flatlander: A person from the prairies.

Folk Fest: Short for the Winnipeg Folk Festival, an annual and international music event that draws about 55,000 people (over four days) to Birds Hill Park just north of Winnipeg.

Goldeye: A freshwater fish found only in Manitoba and usually served smoked; also the name of the professional baseball team — the Winnipeg Goldeyes.

Gotch/gitch: Men's underwear, specifically briefs, and for some reason called gonch in Alberta.

Halloween apples: Greeting used by Manitoba children on Halloween rather than "trick or treat."

Hurry hard: Heard around Manitoba curling rinks, the command to sweep the rock hard and fast down the ice.

Jambuster: A jam-filled doughnut, usually sugar-coated.

Jam (out): To bow out or renege on doing something or going somewhere.

Jeanne's cake: A special cake with a shortbread base made at Jeanne's Bakery in Winnipeg, and consumed at birthday parties and celebrations.

Ladge: Lagimodiere Boulevard, a main artery that runs through Winnipeg and leads to Grand Beach.

L.C.: An abbreviation of MLCC (Manitoba Liquor Control Commission), the government-owned retailer of beer, wine and spirits.

The Leg (pronounced Lej): Short for the Legislative Building.

Matrimonial cake: A date-filled oatmeal dessert slice, called a "date square" in other parts of the country.

Monkey trails: Winding dirt trails in the woods or parks, usually for mountain biking.

Muskie: Nickname for "muskellunge," a large, sharp-toothed freshwater fish similar to the northern pike. "Husky the Muskie," a large statue of the fish, greets people arriving in Kenora, just over the Manitoba-Ontario border.

North of 60: Any place in the province located north of the 60°-N latitude, in other words, way up there.

Out east/back east/down east: May refer to anywhere in Canada east of Thunder Bay, but often refers to Toronto.

Take 5 TOP FIVE ITEMS
ON A UKRAINIAN RESTAURANT MENU

1. **Borscht** – soup made of beets and cabbage, often served with a dollop of sour cream.
2. **Perogies** – fried or boiled dumplings usually stuffed with potatoes and cheese and accompanied by sour cream and onions.
3. **Holubtsi** – tomato sauce covered cabbage rolls stuffed with rice and sometimes meat.
4. **Kolbassa** – a highly seasoned sausage, often served with sauerkraut.
5. **Paska** (Easter bread) and **babka** (desert bread).

Pickerel: Another name for "walleye," a popular freshwater fish particularly plentiful in Lake Winnipeg.

Prairie oysters: A so-called prairie delicacy featuring the testicles of a bull, usually served fried.

Sal's: Nickname for Salisbury House, a Manitoba chain of 24 restaurants famous for its nips (hamburgers) and chips (french fries).

Saskatoon: Not the city in Saskatchewan, but an edible berry found in the prairies, often in wild bushes. The saskatoon is similar to a blueberry, but smaller and with a stronger flavour.

Take 5 — JAKE MACDONALD'S TOP FIVE REASONS FOR NOT CATCHING ANY FISH IN MANITOBA

Jake MacDonald is a Manitoba author, journalist and former fishing guide. His feature writing has appeared in *The Globe and Mail, Maclean's, Canadian Geographic* and *Outdoor Canada*, to name a few, and he is the winner of a number of national writing awards. His best-selling books include *With the Boys, The Houseboat Chronicles*, and the teen novel *Juliana and the Medicine Fish*.

1. **This clear weather has really turned them off**. Fishermen fear a clear blue sky because it signals a high pressure system, which allegedly causes fish to feel moody and menopausal. Fishermen will assure you that this is not some half-baked theory, it's science. Water is not compressible, however (also science), so they haven't determined how fish can feel the atmosphere pressing down on their heads. More research is needed.

2. **This rainy weather has really turned them off**. Fishermen dislike rainy cloudy weather, not just because lightning is attracted to graphite fishing rods, but because low skies and low pressure systems allegedly cause fish to feel moody and menopausal. How fish can feel the lowness of the atmospheric pressure is a matter requiring many beers and much debate.

Sev': Nickname for "7-Eleven," the well-known convenience store.

Shelterbelt: A row of trees at the edge of a farmyard or field, planted to shelter the property from wind and blowing snow.

Smokie: A fat sausage that's a favourite at hot dog stands and on the barbeque.

Social: A party held to raise funds for couples getting married, charities or sports teams. Usually involves cheap liquor, dancing, and light refreshments.

3. **The water is really heating up**. A careful fisherman always tests the temperature of the water with his thermometer before venturing out on the lake. Warm water causes fish to feel sluggish, a bad thing. On a hot day with slow fishing, a wise fisherman will drink many cool beverages to avoid dehydration.

4. **The water is really cooling down**. It's a well known scientific fact that cold weather makes all creatures sluggish. They become less active as the temperature drops. During the winter they barely move, resting in one position for hours on end, with only the slow movement of their chests and the occasional movement of the channel changer indicating they are alive. Fish also slow down quite a bit.

5. **You should have been here last week**. This explanation was used for many years by northern Manitoba fishing guides to explain why guests who travelled fifteen hundred miles and spent as many dollars on that "trip of a lifetime" had failed to catch anything larger than a banana. It fell out of popular use after the Supreme Court of Canada recognized it as an aggravating factor in a highly controversial strangulation case. Nowadays it is popular mainly with cottagers, who use it to good effect on city friends who drop in for the weekend.

Stubble jumper: Someone from the prairies, refers to the vast fields of stubble after the crops have been harvested.

Supper: Refers to the evening meal in rural areas; "dinner" refers to the noon-hour meal. However, urbanites generally call the midday meal "lunch," and the evening one "dinner."

The Fish Bowl: Nickname for CanWest Global Park, the baseball stadium and home of the Winnipeg Goldeyes.

The 'Peg: Short for Winnipeg.

Take 5 BRAD OSWALD'S FIVE MOST THREADBARE WINNIPEG CATCH PHRASES

Brad Oswald is a Winnipeg writer and comedian. As resident television critic at the *Winnipeg Free Press*, he actually gets paid for lying on the couch in his pajamas, eating cereal for lunch and watching TV.

1. **"Yeah, but it's a dry cold."** Winnipeggers have a love-hate relationship with their extreme winter weather — they hate having to deal with it for nearly five months a year, but they're quietly proud as heck of being able to survive in one of the most frigid urban centres on the planet. "Dry cold" comes out anytime someone from winter-damp Toronto makes fun of the 'Peg's too-cold-to-be-cool climate.

2. **"I can get it wholesale."** Again, a manifestation of Winnipeggers' deeply conflicted sense of self; they want to be treated like big-city folks, but blanch at the notion of paying big-city prices. Everybody in Winnipeg knows somebody who can get them a deal on whatever it is they're trying to buy. Retail is for rubes; 'Peg people are, well, cheap.

3. **"Friendly Manitoba."** The familiar license-plate lettering might well be the most ironically ill-conceived automotive slogan in history. Winnipeggers may, indeed, be friendly folk, but put them behind the wheel of a car, and they're downright discourteous. Stop signs are nothing more than a suggestion, and amber lights at intersections are an invitation for you, you, you and three more after that to barrel through after yellow turns to red. Winnipeg is also the only

The Phone Booth: Nickname for the MTS (Manitoba Telecom Services) Centre, a large entertainment complex and hockey arena in downtown Winnipeg.

The Rez: A First Nations reserve, particularly the residential part.

'Toban: Refers to a Manitoban, often heard in northwest Ontario.

Uke: A Ukrainian.

Winterpeg: Nickname for Winnipeg, in reference to its longest, coldest season.

---

place on earth where a lane-change signal light creates an immediate impulse to accelerate, close the gap and deny the merge.

4. **"Bring back the Jets!"** Winnipeg's puck-proud populace has never recovered from the loss of its beloved NHL franchise to those devilish denizens of the Arizona desert. Every time a southern-US team falters, somebody revives the suggestions that the Jets, or a team by some other moniker, should put Winnipeg back in The Show. The simple fact of the matter is that the 'Peg couldn't fill the barn for 40-plus home games at current NHL prices. So, like, let it go. Move on. Embrace the AHL Moose.

5. **"--------- Capital of Canada"** You name it, Winnipeggers want to lay claim to being the best, worst, biggest, baddest, longest, fattest, friendliest, smartest, coldest, hottest, thirstiest, scariest and pretty-much-anything-else-est in the entire country. Murder capital? Yep, and we get pretty ticked if some other burg chalks up more per-capita killings in a year. Slurpee capital? Of course, and it's not just the slushy beverage treats that are causing a collective brain freeze. Car-theft capital? It's part of what drives us. But you know what? It's actually OK to be from a pretty average, pretty mid-sized city with a funny name that gets made fun of on *The Simpsons*. Just be yourself, Winnipeg; you'll be fine.

Natural World

Close to the geographic centre of North America and known as the "Keystone Province," Manitoba conjures up images of endless flat, sweeping plains and a big flood-prone river. This is true of the south central part of the province; however, that terrain exists in less than one-third of Manitoba. Head north and you'll discover that 60 percent of Manitoba is a rugged often remote landscape of forests, connected by a vast system of rivers and lakes, some of which rank among the largest freshwater bodies in the world. As one approaches the far north of the province, the trees end and permafrost begins where sub-Arctic tundra meets the coast of the Hudson Bay.

The Canadian Shield, which underlies much of the north, is most evident in the eastern part of the province where it combines with dense coniferous forests and clear lakes to offer prime cottage country and parkland. This region stands in contrast to the parkland of the southwest, where the prairies stretch out into rolling hills and the woods are filled with spruce and aspen.

GEOGRAPHIC ORIGINS

The easternmost of the three prairie provinces, Manitoba is comparatively level, with elevations generally ranging from 150 m to 300 m above sea level. Manitoba's terrain is varied; however, as the northern three-fifths of Manitoba consists of the Precambrian rock of the Canadian Shield, and more than 15 percent of the province is inland water. The Shield's southern boundary runs east to west just south of Flin Flon, and along the east side of Lake Winnipeg. The transition to the boggy Hudson Bay Lowlands features gentle topography and vegetation.

The geography of Manitoba is largely the product of that ancient and great force of nature — glaciation. In the last ice age, 75,000 to 80,000 years ago, all of Manitoba was covered by ice. When the ice dammed northward-flowing rivers, huge glacial lakes formed. Lake Agassiz, the largest of these, covered much of southern Manitoba and left behind the province's "big three" bodies of water — Lakes Winnipeg, Winnipegosis and Manitoba. The retreat of glacial lakes, and the subsequent lake floors, is also responsible for the legendary flatness of the south, including the Red River Plain.

While most of northern and central Manitoba is a maze of bush and water, the south features a wide tract of agricultural land that lies in a triangle between the borders of Saskatchewan (west), the US (south) and the west shore of Lake Winnipeg. In the southwest corner of the province, bedrock of the Cretaceous Age formed the Manitoba Escarpment and its "mountains" (more like massive, rolling hills) that include Riding Mountain, Duck Mountain, the Porcupine Hills and Turtle Mountain.

LONGITUDE AND LATITUDE
- Northern boundary: 60° north latitude
- Southern boundary: 49° north latitude
- Western boundary: Between 101° 30' and 102° west longitude
- Eastern boundary: 95° west longitude, angling northeast at 53° north latitude

On the global grid, Winnipeg is located at 49° 54' north latitude and 97° 14' longitude. This places it on a similar latitude as Vancouver and Paris, and a similar longitude as Dallas, Texas.

PHYSICAL SETTING

- Size: 649,950 km^2
- Land area: 548,360 km^2
- Water area: 101,593 km^2
- Length: 1,225 km
- Width across the south: 449 km
- Width across the north: 418 km
- Highest elevation: (Mount Baldy) 831 m
- Lowest elevation: Hudson Bay shoreline (sea level)
- Percentage of Canada's total area: 6.5 percent

Sources: Natural Resources Canada, Travel Manitoba.

WATER, WATER EVERYWHERE

- Percentage of the province covered by water: 15 percent
- Approximate number of lakes: 100,000
- Kilometres of coastline: 645 km (Manitoba is the only prairie province with a seaport — Churchill on Hudson Bay)

A RIVER RUNS THROUGH IT

Rivers are central to Manitoba's history and its founding as a province. Aboriginal people, voyageurs, fur traders, early settlers and merchants have travelled Manitoba's waterways from the Hudson Bay south to the US border. Manitoba's rivers have been integral to the region's wildlife, people and economy.

All water in Manitoba flows north into the Hudson Bay, and the province's geological origins and central location on the continent make it "downstream" from many places. Rivers flow into Manitoba from Saskatchewan (the Assinboine and Churchill), the US (the Souris and Red); and Ontario (the Winnipeg, Bloodvein and Berens).

Did you know...

that Assiniboine Forest in Winnipeg is the largest urban nature park in Canada and is home to 80 species of birds?

Take 5   GLENN HALGREN'S TOP FIVE
MANITOBA BEACHES

A former commercial fisherman and resident of Victoria Beach, Glenn Halgren has grown up in and around Manitoba's lakes, beaches and great outdoors. For more than 17 years, he and his wife Cathy have published *The Cottager* magazine, which focuses on cottage country and lake life in Manitoba and Northwestern Ontario.

1. **Elk Island** is part of Grand Beach Provincial Park, located just off the northern tip of Victoria beach on Lake Winnipeg and accessible only by boat. On the west side of Elk Island there's a beautiful, private beach with 40-feet high sand cliffs. If you get tired of lying on the shore, it's also a great place to go beach combing — you never know what you'll find.

2. **Grand Beach**, on the east shore of Lake Winnipeg, 90 km north of Winnipeg, is a famous 3-km stretch of white, powdery sand that is ranked as one of the top 10 beaches in North America.

3. **Winnipeg Beach**, on the southwestern shore of Lake Winnipeg about 55 km north of Winnipeg, is a beautiful sandy beach. The beach and surrounding town were the location for the Global TV series Falcon Beach, filmed in the summers of 2005 and 2006.

4. **Hillside Beach** is a small private beach for cottagers, located 110 km north of Winnipeg on the southeast side of Lake Winnipeg. The water is shallow, making it perfect for small children, and tall meandering dunes back the soft sandy beach. It's one of the best places in all of Manitoba to watch the prairie sunset.

5. **Wachorn Bay**, located on Lake Manitoba near Moosehorn, is a shallow, rocky beach that has some of the clearest blue water in the province. Plus, you can drive on the sand dunes and camp right on the beach!

Take 5 TOP FIVE LARGEST
MANITOBA LAKES

1. **Lake Winnipeg**, 24,400 km²; 6th largest in Canada
2. **Lake Winnipegosis**, 5,370 km²; 11th largest in Canada
3. **Lake Manitoba**, 4,24 km²; 13th largest in Canada
4. **Southern Indian Lake**, 2,015 km²
5. **Cedar Lake**, 1,353 km²

Sources: Canadian Encyclopedia; Encyclopedia of Manitoba.

MAJOR RIVERS

- **The Assiniboine River.** 1,070 km long, it rises in southeastern Saskatchewan and flows southeast across the Manitoba border, where it is joined by the Qu'Appelle River and, southeast of Brandon, the Souris River. It joins the Red River at the Forks in Winnipeg, and then cuts a wide, scenic valley through the Manitoba Escarpment, and drains a broad, fertile plain that supports the province's vast wheat fields.

- **The Red River.** 877 km long, the Red flows north from North Dakota and crosses the Canadian border at Emerson, Manitoba. It meets its major tributary, the Assiniboine, in Winnipeg before it enters Lake Winnipeg. The Red River has the unfortunate habit of flooding when a late spring thaw combined with heavy snow causes it to spill over its shallow banks onto the surrounding plain.

- **The Churchill River.** 1,609 km long, the Churchill originates in northwestern Saskatchewan, flows east across northern Manitoba and empties into the Hudson Bay at the port of Churchill. Along its

Did you know...

that at one point in geological history, Manitoba was an alpine province with huge mountain ranges?

varied route are rapids, falls, narrow chutes and long stretches of smooth water, typical of many rivers of the Canadian Shield. The waterway is historically important as it was travelled by the Cree and Chipewyan, as well as fur traders, early explorers and members of the Hudson's Bay Company.

Ocean on the Prairies

Lake Winnipeg occupies 24,000 km^2 in the middle of Manitoba, and is the 10th largest (by area) body of freshwater in the world. A long (416 km north to south) but comparatively narrow lake, when the wind and waves sweep across the water it can feel, and look, like the high seas.

Although relatively shallow, with an average depth of 12 m, this grand ol' lake is a favourite destination for commercial fishers, sailors, cottagers and tourists. Its white sandy beaches, particularly on the southern shorelines, are among Manitoba's best, and Grand Beach is one of the finest in North America. Lake Winnipeg is also home to 23,000 residents who live in 30 communities along its shoreline.

This massive lake drains 984,000 km^2 of land, by way of Saskatchewan, Alberta and northwest Ontario, as well as most of southern Manitoba and parts of Minnesota and North Dakota. As an unfortunate result, pollution and wastewater arrive from a wide range of sources — farms, industry, cities, towns and recreational areas. In recent years, sewage, fertilizers, chemicals and other contaminants have compromised the lake's environmental health and water quality. In particular, the increasing number of toxic algae blooms has raised concern among biologists, ecologists and area residents. The provincial government, and groups such as the Lake Winnipeg Research Consortium, are monitoring the lake's water quality, and have introduced regulations to reduce levels of phosphorus and nitrogen.

With its many bays, beaches, harbours and points, Lake Winnipeg is 1,750 km of amazing shoreline, a small "ocean on the prairies" that is one of Manitoba's star attractions.

Take 5 — TOP FIVE MOST POPULAR
GAME FISH IN MANTIOBA

1. **Walleye**
2. **Trout**
3. **Northern Pike**
4. **Channel Catfish**
5. **Bass**

Source: Canadian Encyclopedia.

- **The Hayes River.** The Hayes measures 483 km and flows northeast through the rock and bush of the Canadian Shield, across the Hudson Bay Lowlands and into the Bay at York Factory. The river, named for Sir James Hayes, a charter member of the Hudson's Bay Company, was the primary route for First Nations people and fur traders between Lake Winnipeg and York Factory for nearly 200 years. The Hayes is now part of the Canadian Heritage Rivers System, and is one of the few major rivers in North America that remains in a wild, unaltered state.

PARKS
- Park land: 4.85 million hectares
- Number of provincial parks: 80
- Area of provincial parks: 3.41 million hectares
- Number of federal parks: 2
- Heritage parks: 7
- Recreation parks: 51

PROTECTED AREAS
- Park reserves: 14
- Ecological reserves: 21
- Wildlife management areas: 46
- Provincial forests: 2

Sources: Manitoba Conservation – Parks and Natural Areas; Parks Canada.

Take 5
TOP FIVE MOST COMMON TREE SPECIES

1. **Black Spruce**
2. **White Spruce**
3. **Jack Pine**
4. **Tamarack**
5. **Aspen**

Sources: Encyclopedia of Manitoba; Manitoba Conservation.

Birds Hill Provincial Park: Just 24 km north of Winnipeg, this park includes a large man-made lake and beach area, easy hiking trails through woods of oak and aspen, and paved cycling trails. In July, it is the site of the internationally renowned Winnipeg Folk Festival.

Hecla/Grindstone Provincial Park: Located in Manitoba's Interlake, Hecla/Grindstone has acres of forest, a rugged shoreline and plenty of wildlife. Hecla Island was settled by Icelandic immigrants in the 1870s, and is now the site of the new five-star Hecla Oasis Resort and spa, as well as an 18-hole golf course, marina, beach and campground area.

Nopiming Provincial Park: In the east part of the province in Canadian Shield country, Nopiming features towering granite outcrops, more than 700 lakes and sprawling forests of black spruce. There are also campgrounds and a wide array of fishing lodges.

Whiteshell Provincial Park: About 125 km east of Winnipeg, the Whiteshell is the oldest and one of the largest (2,590 km^2) provincial parks. It contains 200 lakes, beautiful waterfalls, and a raft of fishing lodges and both summer and winter resorts. Falcon Lake and West Hawk Lake are found here, along with several hiking trails, including the 66 km Mantario Trail.

Spruce Woods Provincial Park: Just south of Carberry, Spruce Woods is a Natural Park that preserves the delta and sand hills created by glacial Lake Agassiz. The 25 km of sand dunes, called the "Spirit Sands" are the only part of the park not reclaimed by spruce trees. There's a self-guided hiking trail through the desert-like sand hills, and you can see a variety of wildlife, including some reptiles and amphibians.

Riding Mountain National Park: Located in western Manitoba, this 2,973 km^2 expanse of parkland was established in 1929, and is the second oldest national park in Canada. Riding Mountain dominates the east half of the park, while the western part consists of boreal and mixed forest, open meadows and prairie. The park features 200 species of birds as well as elk, moose and bison.

Wapusk National Park: Manitoba's lesser known national park is in the far north; it encompasses a large area of the Hudson-James Lowlands natural region that borders on Hudson Bay. The park's landscape moves from boreal forest to Arctic tundra. Wapusk means "White Bear" in Cree, an appropriate name as the park protects one of the world's largest known polar bear maternity denning areas.

WOODLAND

Trees cover approximately 26.3 million of the province's hectares. Boreal (Northern Coniferous) forest dominates, covering a broad swath of the north-central and central parts of the province, extending east to the Ontario border. Mixed-wood forest, known as aspen parkland, is found in south-central Manitoba, and features an abundance of aspen as well as smaller amounts of white spruce, oak, maple and elm. About 59 percent of Manitoba forests are softwood, 20 percent mixed-wood and 21 percent hardwood.

Source: Government of Manitoba.

MOTHER NATURE'S PRUNING

Trees cover two-fifths of Manitoba, and that makes for a whole lot of firewood. The forest fire season lasts from April to October, and on average 544 forest fires burn about 432,000 hectares per year. In 2007, 382 fires blazed through 336,281 hectares of Manitoba woods. The worst forest fire season in recent history was 1989, when 1,226 fires scorched 3,567,947 hectares.

Take 5 PAUL BROWNE'S TOP FIVE
MANITOBA NATURAL SITES TO PHOTOGRAPH

Paul Browne is a well-known nature photographer who has been travelling throughout Manitoba for more than 25 years capturing its stunning natural wonders. His images have appeared in *Canadian Geographic, Canadian Wildlife* and *Harrowsmith*, among many magazines and books.

1. **Riding Mountain National Park** is a 4½ hour drive northwest of Winnipeg, and lies perched 500 m above the surrounding farmland on the Manitoba escarpment. Its beautiful landscapes and abundant wildlife are a nature photographer's dream come true.

2. **Tulabi Falls, in Nopiming Provincial Park** is about 2 hours northeast of Winnipeg in Canadian Shield country and features beautiful scenery and abundant wildlife. Tulabi Falls and Tulabi Lake are personal favorites, especially viewed from the overlook high on the cliffs of Tulabi Lake.

3. **Steep Rock on Lake Manitoba** is about 3 hours straight north of Winnipeg on Highway 6. Steep Rock offers wonderful views of Lake Manitoba from its elevated limestone cliffs.

4. **Pembina Escarpment** is about 1½ hours southwest of Winnipeg where it rises dramatically from the surrounding prairie landscape. Its rolling hills and beautiful vistas are especially beautiful in autumn.

5. **Oak Hammock Marsh** is just a half-hour north of Winnipeg off Highway 67. Oak Hammock is a bird watchers paradise. Situated on a major migration flyway, one can see a vast assortment of species as they make their way north and south. Tens of thousands of geese are the highlights during spring and fall.

They Said It

"Manitoba is all about diversity and natural splendour — Canadian Shield, boreal forest, luxuriant river valleys, arctic tundra and the prairies potholes."

– Bill Stilwell, author of *Manitoba, Naturally – Scenic Secrets of Manitoba*, 2006.

BRING IN THE SWAT TEAM

Manitoba has the dubious distinction of being Canada's mosquito capital. Nearly 50 different species of mosquitoes buzz around the province, but in the summer it feels like a lot more. The annoying abundance of these insects is explained by the high number of species in Manitoba, their adaptive diversity, and the ideal mosquito living conditions that prevail in wet low-lying parts of the province. Humans are definitely outnumbered: one hectare of northern Manitoba muskeg, or bog, can produce more than 10 million mosquitoes during the short summer. And city dwellers are not immune — Winnipeg has its own entomologist, and spends several million dollars yearly on various chemical and biological means of combating the stinging pests.

SMOKED FISH, A FAVOURITE DISH

Manitoba's most celebrated freshwater fish, the goldeye, is small (about 450 grams) but tasty. It is an important commercial fish that is smoked and sold as a delicacy. Goldeye can be found in the province's major waterways and lakes, from the Red and Assiniboine Rivers to the headwaters of the Churchill and Nelson Rivers. Winnipeg's Goldeyes baseball team is named after this favourite fish.

Did you know...

that Manitoba has the highest per capita ownership of cottages in Canada, with approximately 35,000 cottages located in rural municipalities or provincial parks? Lake Winnipeg is a particularly popular vacation spot.

Take 5

TOP FIVE BIRDS
TO WATCH IN MANITOBA

1. **Great Gray Owl** (boreal forest)
2. **Ross's Gull** (Churchill)
3. **Baird's Sparrow** (extreme southwest Manitoba)
4. **Yellow Rail** (Douglas Marsh)
5. **Connecticut Warbler** (southern fringe of the boreal forest)

Source: Manitoba Naturalists Society.

BEARS & BELUGAS

While Manitoba is home to thousands of black bears, it's the great white ones up north that get all the press. People travel from around the globe to visit the area near Churchill which is home to the world's largest concentration of polar bears. The bears are often seen along the coastal tidal flats of Hudson Bay during the late summer and fall, and have been known to roam through town. While most Manitobans have never laid eyes on a polar bear in the wild, *ursus maritimus* is nonetheless a powerful symbol of the province, and of Canada. Unfortunately, polar bear numbers are declining, and the bear population of the western Hudson Bay region, which extends from the Manitoba-Ontario border to Nunavut's Chesterfield Inlet, is now less than 1,000.

For those who prefer whale watching to scoping for bears, Hudson Bay is also home to beluga whales. Each summer, the mammals return to the estuaries of the Nelson, Churchill and Seal rivers to feed and calve. Many travel companies offer special tour packages to Churchill to see bears, whales and other arctic wildlife.

Did you know...

that the world's largest statue of a mosquito is a roadside attraction in Komarno, Manitoba? "Komarno" means "full of mosquitoes" in Ukrainian.

Take 5 TOP FIVE MANITOBA
HIKING TRAILS

1. **Hunt Lake Trail** – Whiteshell Provincial Park
2. **Grey Owl Cabin Trail** – Riding Mountain National Park
3. **Epinette Creek Trail** – Spruce Woods Provincial Park
4. **Spirit Sands Trail** – Spruce Woods Provincial Park
5. **Elk Island Hike** – Lake Winnipeg, north of Victoria Beach

Source: Manitoba Naturalists Society.

ENDANGERED ANIMALS

All of Manitoba's endangered species are birds, although other animals including the polar bear, the great plains toad and the mule deer fall under the "Threatened" category. For some species, like the grizzly bear, musk ox, and greater prairie chicken, it's too late — these animals have been extirpated and are no longer found in the province.

MANITOBA'S ENDANGERED ANIMALS

- Baird's Sparrow
- Burrowing Owl
- Eskimo Curlew
- Loggerhead Shrike
- Peregrine Falcon
- Piping Plover
- Ross's Gull
- Uncas Skipper
- Whooping Crane

Source: Government of Manitoba - Manitoba Conservation.

TOP FIVE AGRICULTURAL ANIMALS
(MILLIONS OF ANIMALS, 2006)

1. Hens and chickens	7.89
2. Pigs	2.93
3. Cattle & calves	1.57
4. Turkeys	.68
5. Beef cows	.66

Source: Manitoba Conservation.

FARM COUNTRY

In 2006, about 7.7 million hectares were cleared for agricultural use. The total number of farms in the province was 19,054, with an average farm size of 405 hectares. About 61 percent of farmland was devoted to crops, 27 percent was used for pasture land and 2 percent was left fallow.

RULES OF OWNERSHIP

In Manitoba, there is no limit on the amount of farmland that Canadian (permanent) residents can own. Non-residents are restricted to 5 acres or less, but may apply to the Farm Protection Board for an exemption that allows them to own more land in certain cases.

Weblinks

Manitoba Conservation

www.gov.mb.ca/conservation

The Province of Manitoba's website for information about Manitoba forestry, fire programs and environmental issues, as well as species at risk.

Manitoba Parks

www.gov.mb.ca/conservation/parks

A branch of Manitoba Conservation, this site offers information about facilities and services in Manitoba parks. The site features information on nature programs and workshops and environmental action, as well as topics including hiking trails, birds and prairie grass.

Manitoba Naturalists Society

www.manitobanature.ca

This not-for-profit association focuses on the popular and scientific study of nature in Manitoba. The site features information on indoor and outdoor nature programs, workshops and environmental action, as well as books and brochures on topics including hiking trails, tall grass prairie and the birds of Manitoba.

Place Names

Manitoba's place names reflect the rhythm of her native languages, the stories of her pioneers and the legends of her past. Many names originate from the First Nations people who have called Manitoba home for millennia, or are from the explorers, settlers, government and business leaders who opened this gateway to the west and established many of the communities of the Keystone Province. Other names refer to Manitoba's geography — particularly the plentiful lakes, rivers and beaches that are central to the area's natural history and physical beauty.

Altona: This Pembina valley town was named for a suburb of Hamburg, Germany, and Altona translated in English means "all too close." Mennonites from the Ukraine settled the area in 1874 and 1875.

Arborg: The name of this village northwest of Gimli means "town by a river," which refers to the nearby Icelandic River.

Ashern: With the arrival of the railway in 1911, this village in Manitoba's Interlake was named after A.S. Hern, a railway timekeeper.

Beausejour: Southeast of Selkirk, this town may have earned its French name from one of two legends. The first says French voyageurs upon discovering the beauty of the campsite exclaimed, "What a fine day," while the more accepted version claims a French railway engineer decided this high grassy plain was a "beausejour," or in English "a good stopping place."

Berens River: Located on the east side of Lake Winnipeg, the village takes its name from the river that flows west into the lake, and honours Joseph Berens, governor of the Hudson's Bay Company from 1812-22.

Bissett: This former mining town northeast of Winnipeg on Rice Lake, is named after Edgar D.R. Bissett, a Member of Parliament for the constituency of Springfield in the 1930s. Gold was discovered here in 1911, and the town is the site of the historic San Antonio Gold Mine.

Boissevain: Originally known as Cherry Creek, the name was changed to honour Adolph Boissevain, a prominent financier who introduced CPR shares to Europe. Located about 65 km south of Brandon near the US border, the town acts as the entrance to the International Peace Gardens.

Brandon: Also known as "the Wheat City," Manitoba's second-largest city gets its name from the Hudson Bay trading post, Brandon House, originally built at the junction of the Souris and Assiniboine rivers in 1793. Brandon House was named in honour of the Duke of Brandon, an ancestor of Lord Selkirk. Brandon is 197 km west of Winnipeg.

Carberry: This CPR railway site was named for Carberry Tower in Musselburgh, Scotland — the seat of Lord Elphinstone. The Lord was an early director of the CPR. The area is also home to the Carberry sand hills, a unique Manitoba landscape.

Carman: This town southwest of Winnipeg was the site of the first Methodist and Protestant church in southern Manitoba west of the Red River; Rev. Dr. Albert Carman dedicated the building and the settlement was named in his honour.

Churchill: Manitoba's northern seaport, located on the west coast of Hudson's Bay at the mouth of the Churchill River, was originally called Munk's Harbour, after the ill-fated sea captain who discovered the port in 1619. The current name derives from Fort Churchill, one of three Hudson Bay forts by the same name in the area between 1685 and 1782. John Churchill, a governor of HBC, later became the Duke of Marlborough. Churchill is Manitoba's oldest community, and boasts the world's largest concentration of polar bears.

Dauphin: North of Brandon nestled in the heart of the Parkland region, this town gets its name from French explorer Pierre Gaultier de Varennes, Sieur de la Vérendrye who established the Fort Dauphin trading post in 1741. Dauphin was the oldest son of the king of France. Today, the town has a large Ukrainian population and hosts Canada's National Ukrainian Festival every August.

Emerson: Located south of Winnipeg on the Manitoba-North Dakota border, this town was named by one of its founders, W.N. Fairbanks, who admired the writer Ralph Waldo Emerson. The town's other founding father, Thomas Carney, invented the cash register.

They Said It

"The licence plate says 'Friendly.' It should also say 'Undervisited,' 'Underappreciated,' and 'Undiscovered,' even by the people who live within its borders."

– **Bartley Kives**, *Winnipeg Free Press* **reporter and author of** *A Daytripper's Guide to Manitoba.*

Flin Flon: This northern copper mining community was named after fictional character Josiah Flintabbatey Flonatin , a statue of whom, designed by cartoonist Al Capp, greets visitors to the town. Flin Flon sits on the Manitoba-Saskatchewan border, about 740 km north of Winnipeg.

Take 5 AL SIMMONS'S TOP FIVE
MANITOBA EXTREMES

Juno Award winner Al Simmons has been in the entertainment business for more than 38 years. The popular Manitoba-based children's performer is one of Canada's most versatile (and extreme) comedians. His off-the-wall performances featuring bizarre gadgets, wild costumes, unique songs and crazy vaudeville-inspired routines are childlike in their inspiration but sophisticated in their execution. Al and his wife, Barbara, have been married for 32 years and have raised their three sons, Karl, Will, and Brad, in harmony and pandemonium near the small, eastern Manitoba town of Anola.

1. **West Hawk Lake**. A hundred million years ago, a meteor crashed into the Canadian Shield and formed an ideal swimming hole. West Hawk Lake is so deep that the water hardly warms up in the summer. I happen to love swimming in clear cold water. The fiery beginning and chilly ending make for an extremely good swim.

2. **Lake Manitoba**. There are places in Manitoba where you can genuinely feel one with nature, as if you were the first person to have ever witnessed the scenery -- even though you know that for thousands of years people have felt exactly the same way. Simply watch a thunderstorm roll across the prairie, walk along East Grand Beach, or better yet visit the virgin Boreal Forest of Black Island on Lake Manitoba.

Gillam: North of the 56th parallel in eastern Manitoba, the village was named for 17th century settlers, Hudson's Bay Company Captain Zachary Gillam and his son, Benjamin, who established the fur trade and land rights here.

3. **Roseisle**. Anyone who thinks Manitoba is flat and boring need only head to the banks of what was once glacial Lake Agassiz on the Manitoba Escarpment in the Roseisle area for X-tremely good X-country skiing.

4. **Kettle Rapids.** Head up toward Churchill and when you've almost run out of road, you will cross the Nelson River. That is where you will see an extremely outrageous road sign. When I was last on tour in Northern Manitoba, the big green highway sign announcing "Kettle Rapids" was decorated with about 20 kettles hung by their cords. Oh yes, and for an added laugh -- one toaster.

5. **Churchill.** Churchill, Manitoba generally brings thoughts of polar bears and beluga whales, but it is the intense sun during the long summer days and the extreme darkness of winter that I love. I want to watch the ravens play on the smooth worn Precambrian rocks, and listen to the waves, and I long to lie on my back in a snow bank, breath the crisp, clean, cold air and watch the Northern Lights fill the entire sky with their psychedelic dance. And since I'm talking about extremes, I'll go to the extreme of giving you one more . . .

5½ **Home**. Just let me stay home and make a pot of soup and be with my family, and I'll be extremely happy.

Gimli: 89 km north of Winnipeg on the west shore of Lake Winnipeg, Icelandic settlers who landed here in 1875 named the site "The Great Hall of Heaven." Formerly known as New Iceland, Gimli was the parent colony for many Icelandic communities in Canada.

Grand Rapids: About 400 km north of Winnipeg, the village takes its name from the once rushing rapids of the Saskatchewan River, now tamed by a hydroelectric dam. The rapids also spawned the first tramway in western Canada which was built in 1874 to enable passengers and freight to bypass the turbulent waters.

 Take 5 FIVE BIG NAME
WRITERS AND MUSICIANS FROM SMALL PLACES

1. **Margaret Laurence, Neepawa, 1926 (died 1987)**. Novelist; Companion of the Order of Canada, Laurence won numerous literary awards and is author of *A Jest of God*, *The Diviners* and *The Stone Angel*, among other books.
2. **Tom Cochran, Lynn Lake, 1953**. Multi-Juno award winning rock musician; Officer of the Order of Canada.
3. **Loreena McKennitt, Morden, 1957**. Celtic musician; Member of the Order of Canada and the Order of Manitoba, winner of Billboard and Juno awards.
4. **Miriam Toews, Steinbach, 1964**. Novelist; winner of the Governor General's Award for *A Complicated Kindness* and author of other acclaimed books.
5. **James Ehnes, Brandon, 1976**. Classical violinist; Grammy and Juno Award winner, and youngest person elected to the Royal Society of Canada.

Killarney: Originally known as Oak Lake when the first settlers arrived in 1880, land surveyor John O'Brien thought the picturesque lake and its surroundings deserved a more beautiful name. The luck of the Irish prevailed, and he succeeded in changing the town's name to Killarney, in honour of the lakes in Kerry, Ireland.

Lynn Lake: This northern town rich in copper and nickel is named after Lynn Smith, chief engineer for the Sherritt Gordon Mining Company at the time it set up operations here in 1947.

Minnedosa: Located in the river valley west of Neepawa, the town derives its name from the Sioux word, *Minnedosa*, which translates as "flowing water." In the early 1880s, settler and sawmill owner J.S. Armitage suggested the name. Previously, the community was known as Tanner's Crossing.

Morden: About 120 km southwest of Winnipeg, this town was named for settler Alvey Morden, who arrived here from Ontario in 1874. Manitobans know it as home to the annual corn and apple festival.

Morris: Directly south of Winnipeg on the Red River, the town was first named Scratching River. Its current name honours Alexander Morris, the second lieutenant governor of Manitoba. Because of its location, Morris was also an early stopping point for stagecoaches and steamships.

They Said It

"With the thermometer at 30 below zero and the wind behind him, a man walking on Main Street in Winnipeg knows which side of him is which."

– Stephen Leacock

Neepawa: The name refers to the Chippewa Indian word, *Neepawa*, which means plenty or abundance. Surrounded by grain fields, the town has adopted the cornucopia or horn of plenty as its emblem.

Winnipeg

Manitoba's capital sits strategically at the confluence of the Red and Assiniboine Rivers and is in the geographic centre of North America. Archeological evidence suggests Aboriginal people have been meeting at the forks of these two rivers for thousands of years. The city's name refers to the Cree words "win" meaning muddy, and "nipee" indicating water.

Once the largest city between central Canada and the west coast (and the third-largest in the country after Toronto and Montreal) Winnipeg is the ninth largest census metropolitan area in Canada with 712,700 people, trailing Toronto, Montreal, Vancouver, Ottawa, Calgary, Edmonton, Quebec City and Hamilton.

In 1738, Pierre Gaultier de Varennes, Sieur de la Vérendrye arrived at this geographically important site to establish a trading post and expand the fur trade. He was the first of many Europeans, including a group of Scottish pioneers who established the first permanent settlement in 1812. Then known as the Red River Settlement, the city grew around two Hudson's Bay Company trading posts, Upper Fort Garry and Lower Fort Garry (located north of the present-day city). In 1873, Winnipeg was incorporated as a city with a population of 1,869. That changed dramatically when the arrival of the Canadian Pacific Railway in 1885 fostered a wave of immigration to the prairies. During this period of unparalleled economic growth and prosperity, Winnipeg became known as "The Gateway to the West."

At the turn of the 20th century, Winnipeg's position as a transportation hub, as well as high wheat prices and increasing agricultural productivity, made the city a boomtown and the wholesale,

Norway House: Located 480 km north of Winnipeg, this community was named after a group of Norwegians who came here to build a road from York Factory to the Red River Settlement. Historically, Norway House held a strategic position in the fur trade at the junction of routes from the north and west.

administrative and financial centre of western Canada. The heart of Winnipeg's commercial activity was at its most famous intersection: Portage and Main. The late 1800s and early 1900s saw the construction of some of the Canadian west's biggest warehouses, as well as skyscrapers and the stunning terra-cotta buildings that still stand in the city's Exchange District. This area takes its name from the Winnipeg Grain Exchange, and was designated a National Historic Site in 1997.

Winnipeg's economic and urban development boom made it one of the fastest growing cities in North America, resulting in the nickname, "Chicago of the North." In addition, some of the Windy City's architects came to practice in Winnipeg, and many of the city's early builders were influenced by the Chicago style. Winnipeg's exponential growth came to an end with the completion of the Panama Canal in 1914, which drastically altered its position as a transportation centre. The economic after effects of WWI, low grain prices and the Depression further restrained Winnipeg's growth.

Winnipeg has a dubious reputation as a place of bone-chilling winters (hence the nickname "Winterpeg"), and mosquito-infested summers. Still, this ethnically diverse and artistic prairie town is one of North America's best kept secrets. Winnipeg has a thriving cultural scene that includes the Royal Winnipeg Ballet and other dance companies, as well as vibrant visual arts, music and literary communities. Winnipeg is also home to several professional theatre companies, and the city hosts two of Canada's most unique festivals – the Winnipeg Folk Festival and Le Festival du Voyageur.

Pine Falls: This pulp and paper town's name refers to the northern forest and waterfalls, which are east of the community. Established in 1925, the village grew with the arrival of the Manitoba Pulp and Paper Mill.

Take 5 — DOREEN PENDGRAC'S FIVE MOST INTRIGUING MANITOBA TRAVEL EXPERIENCES

Winnipeg-born Doreen Pendgracs is now based in Matlock. A well-travelled professional freelance writer, she has been writing travel articles about intriguing places for North American publications since 1995. Doreen has visited about 30 countries and is still amazed by Manitoba's wonders.

1. A visit to the **Manitoba Legislative Buildings** to uncover the Hermetic Code: Yes, we have our own mysterious Da Vinci Code right here in the provincial capital! Secret codes and reasons for all the intricate designs are found throughout the Manitoba Tyndall Stone building. Read the book (*The Hermetic Code*) or take the tour to learn more.

2. **Morden's Canadian Fossil Discovery Centre:** Where else can you go in Manitoba and be greeted by a life-sized, multi-toothed mosasaur and tylosaur? The remarkable fossils (all found locally) date to 80 million years ago!

3. **York Factory:** Don't wait to visit this one as the main building is sinking into the Hayes River and will probably be gone within 70 years — incredible history literally slip sliding away. The massive oak plank building was once a depot for the Hudson's Bay Company, and is now a National Historic Site. York Factory is only open for special tours -- getting to where the Hayes River meets Hudson Bay is really quite the challenge!

4. **Churchill:** Why is it that most of the tourists you meet in Churchill are from parts of the world other than Manitoba? Churchill features not just polar bears and beluga whales, but also herds of caribou and northern lights like you've never seen before.

5. **Gimli's Icelandic Festival:** I challenge anyone to say "Islendingadagurinn" correctly on the first try! I've been going to this fantastic festival since I was a kid and still can't get it right! And where else can you wear Viking horns on your head without getting funny looks?

Portage la Prairie: The city's name is French for "Prairie Portage." The fur traders crossed this portage to get from the Assiniboine River to Lake Manitoba. By 1870, Portage la Prairie was a village of about 130; it was incorporated as a town in 1881 with the arrival of the CPR, and became a city in 1907.

Roblin: This western Manitoba town's name honours Sir Rodmond Palen Roblin, premier of Manitoba from 1900-15. His grandson, Charles Dufferin ("Duff") Roblin, served as premier of the province from 1958-67.

Russell: Located close to the Manitoba-Saskatchewan border, the town was named by Colonel C.A. Boulton, who participated in the Northwest Rebellion. He named it after General Lord Alexander Russell, commander of the forces in Canada from 1883-88.

Ste. Anne: The first priest who ministered to the Métis in the area, Father LeFloch, came from Brittany and named this village Ste. Anne after the patron saint of that part of France.

St. Laurent: The village on the southeast shore of Lake Manitoba was named by a priest after the Christian martyr Saint Lawrence. The first permanent community was established in 1890, when French families bought land from the Métis.

St. Pierre-Jolys: Located near the Rat River and an important fur trading area in the early days, this community is named for Saint Peter. The second part of the name honours Father J.M. Jolys, the first resident priest in the village and whom many consider its founder.

Selkirk: Situated just northeast of Winnipeg, the town was named for Thomas Douglas, 5th Earl of Selkirk (1771-1820), who established the Red River Settlement in 1812, at the forks of the Red and Assiniboine rivers.

Souris: Located southwest of Brandon at the junction of Plum Creek and the Souris River, the town was called Plum Creek until 1904, when councillors decided to name it after the larger body of water. Souris also boasts the longest suspension bridge in Canada at 177 m.

Sprague: This southern Manitoba village was named for D.E. Sprague, president of a local lumber company; not surprisingly the area is rich in timber.

Steinbach: A short drive east of Winnipeg, this town was established by Mennonite settlers who came from Steinbach, Russia, in 1874. *"Steinbach"* means "stony brook" in German. The town's nickname is "Automobile City" due to its large number of car dealerships.

Stonewall: This town sits just north of Winnipeg and west of Selkirk, and pioneer legend attributes its name to a Mr. Jackson, a postmaster whose nickname was "Stonewall" after the American confederate general. The limestone outcroppings north and east of the town may also have contributed to the name.

Swan River: At one time the centre of a thriving fur trade, this town was once the legislative headquarters of the Northwest Territories (1875), when it was outside the limits of the small province of Manitoba. It takes its name from the white swans that were seen on Thunder Hill nearby.

The Pas: About 600 km northwest of Winnipeg, The Pas is the gateway to Manitoba's north. Of the several possible origins of the town's name, the most widely accepted is that it derives from the Cree word *pasquia*, meaning "narrows between wooded banks." At the junction of the Saskatchewan and Pasquia rivers, La Vérendrye and French voyageurs built Fort Paskoyac here in 1750. In the 1800s, The Pas became a centre for missionary service. The CNR reached The Pas in 1907, and it became part of the newly expanded province of Manitoba in 1912.

Thompson: The northern city known as the nickel capital of Manitoba, takes its name from John F. Thompson, former president of the International Nickel Company. Established around the mining industry, the city rapidly developed in 1956 and a CNR line linking Thompson with the Hudson Bay Railway was completed in 1957.

Virden: About 77 km west of Brandon and the centre of many local oil wells, the town was first known as Gopher Creek, and then Manchester, before it became Virden in 1883. It's believed Virden was named after the home of Lord Mount Stephen of Scotland, some of whose relatives homesteaded in the area.

Winkler: This southern Manitoba town was named for its founder, Valentine Winkler, the provincial minister of agriculture from 1915-20.

Winnipeg Beach: This town and summer resort on the west shore of Lake Winnipeg is named for the huge lake on which it sits. An important recreational area, the CPR reached the lakeside community in 1902, and Winnipeg Beach was incorporated as a village in 1909.

York Factory: The oldest settlement in Manitoba, early explorers Radisson and Groseilliers established the first York Factory in 1684. The port was named for James II, at that time the Duke of York and the governor of the Hudson's Bay Company. Through this gateway to the interior, the famous York boats transported European goods from Hudson Bay to the Red River Settlement.

Weather and Climate

Manitobans have a love-hate relationship with the province's climate. They love the brilliant, sunny days (298 a year) and balmy summers at the lake, but hate the long months of "dry cold" that chill the body, freeze-dry the skin, and make venturing outside a daily exercise in survival.

Manitoba's weather can be summed up in one word — extreme. That includes sub-arctic winter temperatures in which wind chills of -40°C to -45°C are not uncommon, and summer heat waves of 30°C to 35°C that are downright tropical when the humidity kicks in. And don't forget winds that sweep across the plains unchecked, occasionally developing into tornadoes.

Yet in the end, Manitobans wear their weather as a badge of honour — whether it's extreme cold, heat, wind or floods — what doesn't kill them only makes them stronger.

AT A GLANCE
- Warmest month: July (19.5°C daily average temperature)
- Coldest month: January (-17.8°C daily average temperature)
- Wettest month: June (89.5 mm average rainfall)

AND THE WINNER IS …

- **Highest temperature:** 44.4°C at Emerson on July 12, 1936, and St. Albans on July 11, 1936.
- **Lowest temperature:** - 52.8°C at Norway House on January 9, 1899.
- **Windiest day:** Winds gusted at more than 420 km/h as an F5 tornado touched down at Elie on June 22, 2007.
- **Wettest day:** On September 18, 1975, the climate station at Riding Mountain National Park received 217.2 mm of rain.
- **Snowiest day:** On November 18, 1906, Dauphin received 76.2 cm of snow — the greatest one-day snowfall in Manitoba's history.

Source: Environment Canada.

SUNSHINE

Manitoba receives about 2,098 hours of sunshine per year, second only to sunny Saskatchewan, which gets 2,206 light-filled hours annually.

Manitobans can expect to see the sun on 298 days of the year, slightly fewer year-round than in Saskatchewan and Alberta; however, Manitoba skies are clearer, placing first in Canada in the "clearest skies year-round" category.

And although Manitoba winters are cold, they are bright — the province has the second sunniest winters in the country, after New Brunswick.

Did you know...

that Winnipeg has been dubbed "the dandruff capital of the world" by Hill Top Research, a company which performs clinical research on personal and health care products? Hill Top has tested anti-dandruff shampoos at its Winnipeg facility since 1995 — Manitoba's cold dry winters apparently are ideal for the production of the white flaky stuff. Other products guinea pigged at the Winnipeg site include women's dry leg moisturizer and sunscreen.

GROWING SEASON

Frost is the enemy of crops, and consequently Manitoba's growing season is short. In Manitoba's agricultural regions, planting may begin in late April, but usually starts in mid-May; most major crops are harvested by the end of September.

Source: Manitoba Agriculture, Food and Rural Initiatives.

RAIN

Among Canada's 13 provinces and territories, Manitoba ranks as the eighth rainiest, recording an average of almost 350 mm on the rain gauge each year. Slightly wetter than the other prairie provinces (Saskatchewan is tenth and Alberta is ninth) Manitoba hardly feels

Professor Popsicle

Where else but Winnipeg would you find the world's leading authority on freezing to death? Gordon Giesbrecht, Ph.D., until recently a physiologist at the University of Manitoba's Laboratory for Environmental Medicine, has studied the effects of cold on the human body by getting close to the elements, very close. Dr. Giesbrecht plunges into icy water, and exposes his body to sub freezing temperatures in order to better understand the effects of hypothermia and how to survive it. His chilly research has earned him the nickname "Professor Popsicle," and Dr. Giesbrecht has lowered his body temperature below 35°C (95°F), which is the threshold for hypothermia, a numbing 40 times.

Dr. Giesbrecht's studies have provided valuable information to rescuers, doctors and the general public about the effects of cold stress, as well as how to treat hypothermia before reaching a hospital. He also teaches people about what to do when a blizzard hits, advising, "stay in your car. And carry an emergency kit." The good Professor has his feet firmly planted in the snow, but keeps an eye on the heavens as well. In June 2008, Dr. Giesbrecht left his research position at the University of Manitoba to become President of Horizon College & Seminary in Saskatoon.

"damp" compared to the wettest province, Nova Scotia, which receives 1,082 mm of rainfall annually.

Manitoba has about 140 wet days annually, with only two of those receiving more than 25 mm or rainfall. Few Manitobans regularly carry umbrellas.

DIG THIS …

Manitoba is the snowiest prairie province, but ranks only eighth in the country. On average, the province receives 176 cm of snow each year, well behind the 452 cm that first ranked Newfoundland and Labrador typically receives.

Manitoba gets snow on average 74 days a year, compared to the winter wonderland of Quebec, where snow falls on 109 days of the year. The snow does stick around, however, staying on the ground in Manitoba for an average 171 days, placing it sixth in the nation for longest snow cover. That's close to the middle of the (snow) pack, trailing first place Nunavut, which is blanketed with snow 265 days of the year, but well ahead of Nova Scotia, where the white stuff is around for only 87 days on average.

Source: Environment Canada.

Did you know...

that Winnipeg ranks as the world's coldest city among centres with a population greater than 500,000?

Did you know...

that the hottest day in Manitoba occurred on July 11, 1936 when the temperature reached 44.4°C at St. Albans (southeast of Brandon)? This day was part of a famous heat wave that affected the prairies and Ontario, producing the hottest temperatures ever recorded in Manitoba.

NOW THAT'S COLD

On February 5, 2007, the temperature in Winnipeg plummeted to −42.2°C, the coldest day in the city in 31 years. Wind chill values dipped below −50°C (a temperature where exposed flesh freezes in less than two minutes) leading to several cases of frostbite and hypothermia.

When these arctic temperatures occur in southern Manitoba, car batteries die and frozen vehicles are left stranded. Authorities advise residents not to travel, rural schools close and some school bus services are cancelled.

BLIZZARDS

The open areas of the Hudson Bay coast are by far the most susceptible region to blizzards in the province, with an average of six per year in Churchill. According to Environment Canada, a blizzard is characterized by a wind chill of -25°C or less, and snow or blowing snow with winds of more than 40 km/hr. The open, flat regions of southern Manitoba, such as the Portage la Prairie area, Winnipeg and the Red River Valley experience blowing snow far more often than the hilly forested regions around Dauphin, Gimli and The Pas. On average, Winnipeg is hit with a blizzard once every two years.

WINNIPEG BLIZZARDS

In 1935, 53 cm of snow fell from March 3-6, with 38 cm of it arriving on one day, March 4, the greatest one-day snowfall ever for the city. Exactly 31 years later, "The Blizzard of '66" arrived when winds gusted to 113 km/hr and Winnipeg was blanketed with more than 35 cm of snow.

November is fair game for snow in Winnipeg, evidenced by the November 7-9, 1986 storm when 36 cm of snow was accompanied by 90 km plus winds and snowmobiles were a common sight around town.

Still, none of these freezing blasts holds a shovel to the "Blizzard of the Century" from April 4-7, 1997, when 48 cm of snow and ice pellets fell on Winnipeg and winds gusted over 80 km/hr.

HOW LOW CAN IT GO ...

When the wind blows and makes the "real feel" temperature danger-ously low, the wind chill is included in the forecast. In most of south-ern Canada, this happens when the wind chill reaches –25°C, the point at which frostbite becomes a risk.

In colder parts of the country, people have adapted to the more severe conditions. Therefore, Environment Canada issues cold weath-

Take 5 MANITOBA'S TOP FIVE
MEMORABLE TORNADOES

The "worst" tornado is a subjective term — those with the highest wind speeds don't always cause the most injuries or damage. F3 twisters (winds from 253 to 330 km/hr) that touched down in St. Claude in 1984 and Baldur in 2007 produced no deaths, and only minor injuries in St. Claude. However, a F3 tornado that hit Aubigny-Ste. Anne in 1978 caused one death and 20 injuries. Here are some other memorable Manitoba twisters:

1. **Elie, June 22, 2007**. An F5 tornado, the strongest in Canadian history, struck this small town.
2. **Gull Lake, Aug. 5, 2006**. This F2 tornado (winds from 181 to 252 km/h) demolished farms, homes, cottages and trailers in the area. Seven people were injured and one woman was killed.
3. **Rosa, July 18, 1977**. An F4 tornado (winds from 331 to 417 km/h) stripped bark from trees, destroyed three farms and killed three people, including a couple whose home was ripped from its foundation.
4. **Vita, June 19, 1955**. A violent, late afternoon tornado destroyed 20 homes and garages, as well as a store, school and church. No one was killed but 30 were injured.
5. **Portage la Prairie, June 23, 1922**. In one of the most deadly torna-does in Manitoba history, this F2 twister killed, 10 and left 50 injured.
Source: Environment Canada.

er warnings at progressively colder wind chill values the farther you move north. Most of Canada, including southern Manitoba, hears a warning at about –45°C; residents of northern Manitoba (and the Arctic) are warned at –50°C.

Winnipeg ranks fourth (not first) among Canadian cities in greatest number of high wind chill days (-30°C or less) annually, recording about 49 very chilly days a year. Winnipeg trails its Manitoba counterparts, Brandon (50 days) and Thompson (83 days) in the cold weather derby; the top wind chill spot in the country is reserved for Yellowknife, NWT (101 days).

Source: Environment Canada.

WHITE CHRISTMAS

Having a White Christmas in Manitoba is close to a sure thing, as the province has an average of 170 days of snow-cover each year — that's more than 5.5 months. The odds of a white Christmas (defined by Environment Canada as at least 2 cm of snow on the ground) is 98 percent for Winnipeg and 93 percent for Brandon. The odds of a white Christmas in Toronto is 57 percent, and in Vancouver only 11 percent.

Winnipeg's greatest amount of accumulated snow on the ground at Christmas was 80 cm in 1955, and the greatest snowfall recorded on Christmas Day itself in Winnipeg was 9.4 cm in 1938. Other notable Manitoba Christmas Day dustings include 10 cm of snow in Thompson in 1985; and 18 cm of the white stuff in Brandon in 1942.

WIND

While the wind does sweep across the open plains, Manitoba is far from the windiest province or territory, placing sixth in the country (behind Nunavut, PEI, Newfoundland, Nova Scotia and Quebec). Manitoba's average wind speed of 13.9 km/hr is just slightly less than the Canadian average of 14.1 km/hr.

Manitoba has about 23 windy days annually (when winds of 40 km/hr or greater blow for more than an hour), the same as Alberta, and just one more per year than Saskatchewan. None of the prairie provinces can compare to Canada's windiest place, Nunavut, where winds whirl 97 days a year on average.

Surprisingly Winnipeg, notorious for high winds, is only the 12th windiest city in Canada, with a highest average hourly wind speed of 17 km/hr. Regina, SK, and Lethbridge, AB rank fifth and eighth respectively, while the windiest urban centre is St. John's, N.L., with an average wind speed of 23 km/hr.

Take 5 SYLVIA KUZYK'S FIVE MOST MEMORABLE WEATHER EVENTS

Sylvia Kuzyk has been a part of the CTV News team for more than 30 years and started her career at CTV as a weather anchor. She currently co-hosts CTV News at Noon, and is a CTV Skywatch Weather Specialist. One of Canada's first women in broadcasting, she is also one of Manitoba's most familiar faces.

1. **The 1997 "Flood of the Century."** My colleagues and I often worked 14-hour days to bring viewers the latest flood coverage.
2. **The big snowstorm that preceded the "Flood of the Century."** It was a long and nasty storm that lasted from April 4th to 7th, and dumped 48 cm of snow over southern Manitoba. Some of us had to be picked up by snowmobile to get in to work.
3. **The summer of 2005, one of the wettest on record.** We were starting to feel like ducks.
4. **The summer of 2004, the coldest on record.** I encountered a lot of grumpy people that summer ... they just weren't happy with the chilly forecasts.
5. **Standing on Portage and Main doing a live weather hit in December with wind chill values of –40°C.** This was one of my worst weather experiences. Some viewers even called to complain that I shouldn't be standing outside in such cold weather.

They Said It

Winter nights are long, summer days are gone
Portage and Main fifty below
Springtime melts the snow, rivers overflow
Portage and Main fifty below
Portage and Main fifty below

> **– Winnipeg musician Randy Bachman. Excerpted from the song**
> **"Prairie Town" from Bachman's 1993 album *Any Road*.**

WIND POWER

To test Manitoba's capacity for generating wind power, an experimental wind turbine was installed in Churchill in 1981. Costs turned out to be prohibitive, however, and Manitoba's first wind farm wasn't established until 2005 in St. Leon, about 150 km southwest of Winnipeg. St. Leon features 63 wind turbines which stand 80 metres tall and generate 99 megawatts of power. The juice is purchased by Manitoba Hydro and provides enough energy to power about 41,000 homes. Manitoba Hydro has plans to develop 1,000 megawatts of wind power capacity in the province by 2010.

TORNADO ZONE

Tornadoes occur about nine times a year in Manitoba, and the windstorm season runs from April to September, with the greatest tornado frequency occurring in July. Tornadoes are most common in southern Manitoba, but occasionally are reported in boreal forest areas, over water and in the north.

Source: Environment Canada.

CANADA'S STRONGEST TORNADO

On June 22, 2007 Canada's first F5 tornado touched down at 6:25 pm near Elie, a sleepy town 40 km west of Winnipeg. A F5 tornado's winds represent the most powerful in the Fujita intensity-scale, with wind speeds exceeding 420 km/hr. Such storms account for less than one percent of tornadoes worldwide.

The localized 300-metre wide tornado hit southern Manitoba and stayed on the ground for 35 minutes, tracking about 5.5 km, before lifting into the air. Its top wind speed was estimated between 420 and 510 km/hr. The force of the tornado blasted the bark off trees, severed utility poles and lifted an entire house a few hundred metres through the air. The high winds also pushed two semi-trailers off the highway. Fortunately, on that June day many Elie residents were out of town

The Flood of the Century

Manitoba is known for extreme cold, but flooding may be just as big a challenge. Residents of the Red River Valley have been dealing with floods since the early 1800s, including an 1852 submersion in which the Red was described as "a lake studded with houses." Nearly 100 years later, the devastating flood of 1950 swamped Winnipeg, inundating one-eighth of the city as well as 1,660 km^2 in the valley south of Winnipeg. The 1950 flood resulted in the evacuation of 100,000 people, the largest such undertaking in Canadian history. That mid-century flood became the catalyst for the 1960s construction of the Red River Floodway, a 47 km-channel built to divert flood waters into Lake Winnipeg.

The Floodway has proved highly effective and has saved Winnipeg from flooding at least 18 times. While the system is usually able to handle the river's capacity, the Floodway could not entirely mitigate 1997's "Flood of Century" when waters crested at 10.5 metres, about 1.5 metres higher than the 1950 flood. At the crest, the amount of water rushing toward Winnipeg was enough to fill an Olympic-sized pool every second. Without the Floodway, 80 percent of the city would have been under water.

The Red River spilled across southern Manitoba to become the "Red Sea" – covering 2,000 km^2, 40 km across at its widest point.

attending a high school graduation, and others knew to seek shelter in basements. Consequently, there were no injuries or deaths.

The Elie twister was just the opener. The next day, tornadoes ripped through southern and western Manitoba; the most damaging one hit Baldur where wind speeds were between 253 and 330 km/hr. Elsewhere, raging winds snapped more than 200 hydro poles across southern Manitoba, uprooted hundreds of trees in Whiteshell Provincial Park, knocked over several Manitoba Hydro towers and damaged more than 1,000 cottages. It was a weekend to remember with eight tornadoes whipping through the province.

Source: Environment Canada.

Over 27,000 people were evacuated, the Canadian Forces brought in 8,000 personnel, and thousands of volunteers helped sandbag dikes, homes and river properties.

Winnipeg and the Red River Valley are part of a flat and shallow flood plain created by a glacial lake, an unfortunate fact of nature that makes Winnipeg perhaps an ill-advised location for a city. Flooding occurs to some degree each spring on the north flowing Red River as ice upstream blocks the river's flow from the south, and water spills over low banks.

The 1997 flood was caused by frozen saturated soil and a deep snowpack with record high water content. These features, combined with an April snowstorm that dumped half a winter's snowfall in the Red River basin in one weekend, put towns south of Winnipeg underwater. By the time the river's crest reached downtown Winnipeg on May 2, the flood had forced about 28,000 people from their homes.

Unofficial estimates of total damage to public and private property, including replacing infrastructure and flood-proofing, exceeded $450 million. However, damages prevented by flood control works and emergency dikes were estimated at over six billion dollars. The Red River Floodway has since been expanded, and Winnipeg is now protected against a one-in-700-year flood.

WHAT THE HAIL ...

The combination of heat, humidity and jet streams makes hailstorms a part of life on the prairies, but 2007 was a particularly bad year. Intense summer storms smashed crops, battered homes and businesses, and beat up vehicles at a rate not seen in more than a decade. According to the Canadian Crop Hail Association, 2007 Manitoba crop claims topped $14 million and there were nearly 5,000 claims.

Take 5 — **JOHN SAUDER'S TOP FIVE**
QUESTIONS FOR A MANITOBA WEATHER ANCHOR

John Sauder is proud to work at the nation's broadcaster, CBC, as meteorologist, forecaster and weather anchor. He is one of only three Canadian meteorologists to receive the American Meteorological Society's Seal of Approval for Weathercasting, and has a certificate in broadcasting meteorology from Mississippi State University.

1. **Hey! How's the weather?** This one is asked at the mall, at Wal-Mart, at the grocery store ... what they are really saying is, "I watch you on TV and I couldn't think of what else to say, but wanted to say hi anyway." I've learned to understand this question over the years and I've decided it's nice that people want to say hi.
2. **Is it true that next winter is going to be even colder?** I don't really believe in long range seasonal forecasts. While they are quite general, any small change in a weather pattern now makes a huge difference down the road.
3. **My wedding is July 10th at 3 pm. Is it going to rain?** This question is usually asked 10 or more days before the wedding, or on a day when scattered showers are in the forecast. There's no way any forecaster can predict every cloud and every raindrop.
4. **When's it going to cool down?** This is a typical question in July. Come on folks, you've been wanting it to warm up all winter. The heat is finally here, get outside and enjoy it . . . with the proper sun protection of course.
5. **When's it going to warm up?** This is a typical question in January and my usual answer is "May." Then I'll get a little more detailed and give the real answer based on my forecast. Cold spells in January can last a while.

They Said It

> "The most significant natural disaster to strike a Canadian community in the 20ᵗʰ century."
>
> **– A Manitoba government minister talking about the 1997 Red River Flood.**

On August 9, a spectacular hail storm pummeled Dauphin and surrounding areas. The 30-minute barrage produced citrus-sized hailstones, destroyed crops only days away from harvest, and triggered 13,000 claims to Manitoba Public Insurance. Losses were estimated at $53 million, and more than 60 percent of damaged vehicles in Dauphin were total write-offs. Most area buildings had dented roofs and lost shingles, while gardens were shredded and trees stripped bare.

Weblinks

Environment Canada Weather

www.weatheroffice.gc.ca

The place to go for climate information for every Canadian city, province, territory and region. Also the best place to check current weather conditions.

Weather Winners

www.on.ec.gc.ca/weather/winners/intro-e.html

Visit this site to see where your city, province or territory ranks in 70 different weather categories. Part of Environment Canada's weather site.

Did you know...

that during the 1997 flood about 8.1 million sandbags were filled and delivered in the city of Winnipeg? If laid end-to-end in a straight line, the sandbags would stretch from Winnipeg to Vancouver.

Crime and Punishment

1835: The Hudson's Bay Company (HBC) produces the first written laws for the Red River Settlement and appoints a number of men as Justices of the Peace.

1845: Executed for the murder of a fellow Saulteaux Indian, Capinesseweet becomes the first person to hang in Manitoba.

1870: Under the leadership of Captain Frank Villiers of the 2nd Quebec Rifles, 10 soldiers from his regiment and 10 local men form the Mounted Constabulary Force (MCF), the province's first official law enforcement body. The MCF polices the entire province and transfers prisoners from Winnipeg to the first penitentiary, which is located at Lower Fort Garry, 32 km away.

1872: The MCF is renamed the Provincial Police Force (PPF); it subsequently becomes known as the Manitoba Provincial Police (MPP).

1873: A combined courthouse and jail is built on Winnipeg's Main Street at William Avenue.

1874: Winnipeg hires its first Chief of Police, John S. Ingram. Manitoba serves as launching point for the "Great March West," and on July 8 approximately 275 officers and men leave Dufferin to provide law enforcement to present-day southern Alberta.

1874: Joseph Michaud becomes the first Manitoban executed under the jurisdiction of the new Dominion of Canada.

1875: Winnipeg Police Chief John S. Ingram resigns in the wake of his arrest for frequenting a house of prostitution.

1876: A federal penitentiary is built at Stony Mountain.

1881: The Vaughan Street Jail opens in Winnipeg.

1887: Winnipeg police detectives are accused of taking bribes from houses of ill repute.

1899: Professional hangman John Radclive comes to Manitoba to carry out the first executions at the Vaughan Street Jail.

1912: Royal North West Mounted Police (RNWMP) responsibilities are extended to include northern Manitoba.

1913: Winnipeg becomes the first city in North America (and the third in the world) to use a police signal system whereby patrolling officers can communicate with the station on a regular basis, as well as in emergencies.

Did you know...

that children as young as five were once held in Winnipeg's Vaughan Street Jail for truancy? The former prison is now used as a maintenance facility.

1914: Career criminal and former pro wrestler John Krafchenko is arrested in Winnipeg for the murder of the bank manager in the town of Plum Coulee. Krafchenko is tried for murder and subsequently executed.

The Flying Bandit

On March 1, 1966, the Winnipeg International Airport was the site of the largest gold heist in Canadian history. Ken Leishman and his accomplices impersonated Air Canada employees and stole $400,000 worth of gold bullion right off the tarmac. In order to pull off the robbery, the thieves used a stolen Air Canada vehicle and fashioned homemade grounds crew uniforms.

Leishman had planned his caper carefully. From his experience as a pilot, he knew that Winnipeg was the regular transfer point for gold bullion originating in Red Lake, Ontario and destined for the Mint in Ottawa.

Grabbing the gold was one thing, but getting away with the crime turned out to be another. Unlike his 1957 Toronto heist, after which the "Flying Bandit" successfully boarded a plane back to Winnipeg with his loot, this time, the escape plan went awry. Several days after the robbery, Leishman, who was on parole for a failed 1961 robbery, was arrested in Vancouver as he tried to flee to Hong Kong.

Leishman was incarcerated at Headingley Penitentiary, but his winning smile, snappy wardrobe and reputation for non-violence elevated him to the status of folk hero. The Flying Bandit has been the subject of a play, a book and even a one-hour documentary by Winnipeg's Frantic Films.

Ironically, after serving his sentence for the airport caper, the father of seven moved his family to Red Lake, Ontario where he opened a tourist shop and became a local celebrity. At one point he was even elected president of the Chamber of Commerce. In December 1979, the Flying Bandit performed his last feat — while piloting a medical evacuation from Red Lake, he perished when his plane crashed into the Canadian Shield.

Take 5 FIVE CRIMINAL NICKNAMES

1. **John "Bloody Jack" Krafchenko** – bank robber/murderer
2. **Earl "The Strangler" Nelson** – serial killer
3. **Carl "Gunner" McGee** – drugstore robber
4. **Mike "The Horse" Attamanchuk** – safe cracker
5. **Ken "The Flying Bandit" Leishman** – bank/gold robber

Source: Winnipeg Police.

1916: Mrs. Mary Dunn becomes Winnipeg's first official "Woman Police Constable." The 43-year-old Dunn is assigned to the Morality Department with duties that include providing aid to wayward children and women in distress.

1919: The Winnipeg Police force dismisses 252 members who refuse to sign an oath of allegiance during the Winnipeg General Strike. Only 22 members sign the oath. During the strike, Royal North West Mounted Police officers charge down Main Street on horseback to disperse crowds of strikers. One man is killed.

1927: Members of the MPP apprehend serial killer Earl "The Strangler" Nelson, wanted for over 20 murders across North America.

1930: A maximum security provincial correction centre opens at Headingley. The Winnipeg Police Force introduces Canada's first radio equipped patrol cars.

Did you know...

that in 2008, *Maclean's* reported that Winnipeg has the third highest crime rate among Canadian cities, trailing only Regina and Saskatoon? Mayor Sam Katz points out that things have improved since 2006 (the year from which statistics used by the magazine were drawn), yet vows to continue to get tough on crime in Winnipeg.

1932: The Royal Canadian Mounted Police (RCMP) assumes provincial policing responsibilities in Manitoba.

1949: A Royal Commission investigates the Winnipeg police force on charges of police brutality, as well as complaints of prisoners being held incommunicado. The department is cleared of wrongdoing.

1952: Henry Malanik, convicted of murdering a Winnipeg police officer, is the last person hanged in Manitoba.

1959: Thanks to Mayor Stephen Juba, Winnipeg becomes the first city in North America to establish a "999" emergency telephone number (later 911).

Manitoba Provincial Police

Although today the province relies on the RCMP for law enforcement, Manitoba once had its own police force. The "Mounted Constabulary Force" was established in 1871 to police the province and escort prisoners to trial. A year later, the name was changed to "Provincial Police Force," and soon after to "Manitoba Provincial Police" (MPP).

Initially consisting of 24 men, by 1874 the MPP had been reduced to a single member. Understaffing was endemic for the next 40 years, except for a brief period during WWI when a border patrol was hired. The force also obtained uniforms around this time; until then they had relied on badges pinned to their civilian clothes.

By 1920, the MPP was back in force with 42 members scattered about the province in one and two man detachments. The force's duties included stopping the illicit liquor trade and protecting rural communities from US gangsters who robbed banks and otherwise terrorized southern towns. The MPP's tenure ended in 1932 when its force of 85 officers was disbanded and replaced by the RCMP.

1966: Ken "The Flying Bandit" Leishman undertakes Canada's largest gold heist at Winnipeg International Airport.

1968: Winnipeg Police Chief George S. Blow organizes a new Juvenile Division to deal with an increase in youth crime.

Take 5 — MIKE MCINTYRE'S TOP FIVE
EXCUSES HE'S HEARD IN COURT

Mike McIntyre is the justice reporter for the *Winnipeg Free Press*. He also hosts the nationally syndicated "Crime and Punishment" radio show on the Corus Radio Network, is the author of three true crime books, and is on the web at www.mikeoncrime.com. And he's tired of hearing excuses from criminals!

1. **"That child porn wasn't for me — it was for the neighbourhood pedophile."** Clarence Hildebrand told court he began accessing kiddie porn so he could deliver it to a local sex offender who was preying on neighbourhood kids. He claims he thought the lurid images might help keep the creep off the streets. Apparently, calling the cops on the predator never entered his mind. Amazingly, a judge bought his bizarre excuse and gave him a year-long conditional sentence.

2. **"I didn't grope that woman — I was just asking for directions."** Douglas Wayne said he was only trying to get a woman's attention to ask for directions when he tapped her on the backside. But the judge ultimately believed the victim's tale. The woman says Wayne "squeezed" her buttocks and laughed as she stood at a parking meter outside a Winnipeg hospital. Wayne also claimed he mistakenly took a double dosage of anti-anxiety medication that morning and may have been "confused and disoriented" at the time.

3. **"I didn't blow that money — my pregnant wife stole it!"** Talk about an airtight alibi. John Mitchell accused his common law wife of stealing

1968: Manitoba motorists begin to think twice about drinking and driving as the Breathalyzer is introduced, providing an immediate measure of blood alcohol level.

1971: A 19-year-old Cree student, Helen Betty Osborne, is abducted and brutally murdered in The Pas.

$300 from him — money he desperately needed to pay someone back. But when police began investigating his claim, they learned the woman couldn't possibly have been involved. That's because she was in the throes of labour at the time the alleged theft occurred. Mitchell ultimately confessed he spent the money on drugs. He was convicted of public mischief and sentenced to six months in jail.

4. **"I wasn't impaired — I was illiterate!"** Ronald Ducharme beat his impaired driving charge with the most unusual explanation. The Winnipeg man told court he can't read and therefore didn't realize he wasn't supposed to drive while taking Tylenol 3s for his chronic back pain. Police had pulled Ducharme over after receiving several reports of his car swerving all over the road. Ducharme claimed he popped three pills before getting behind the wheel. A judge accepted his explanation and found him not guilty.

5. **"That wasn't an assault — it was just rough sex!"** A Winnipeg man says he was only following his girlfriend's kinky orders when he beat her on the buttocks with a wooden chair leg and spanked her with a leather belt, leaving extensive welts and bruising. But he was ultimately convicted when a judge noted a person can't consent to having bodily harm inflicted on them. He was given a conditional discharge and two years probation.

1977: The Provincial Remand Centre opens in Winnipeg to hold those awaiting trial.

1981: Several members of the Winnipeg Police Force face criminal charges for committing a series of break and enters. Two officers are accused of murdering a man (the brother-in-law of one of them) whom they fear will implicate them in the scandal.

You Got the Wrong Man:
Thomas Sophonow and the
Barbara Stoppel Murder

For years, Thomas Sophonow felt as if he bore the mark of Cain. People saw him as a man who got away with murder, yet his conviction hung on barely more than a thread. In fact, it started with a length of twine.

On December 23, 1981, 16-year-old Barbara Stoppel was found strangled in the washroom of the Winnipeg donut shop where she worked. A witness saw the alleged murderer leave the shop and began chasing him, whereupon the cowboy-hat-wearing suspect dropped the twine used in the crime.

It was this twine that was used to link Sophonow to the murder. Convinced that the particular brand of rope was available only on the west coast, police focused their investigation on British Columbia. Sophonow, a frequent traveler between his home in Vancouver and his hometown of Winnipeg, was identified as a suspect.

The 28-year-old had been in town the night of the murder, and fit the suspect's description. Moreover, a witness came forward and claimed to have seen the same twine used in the murder in Sophonow's vehicle. But it was the testimony of John Doerkson, a jailhouse informant, that sealed Sophonow's fate. In exchange for leniency, Doerkson testified to overhearing Sophonow confess to the crime.

1981: A 16-year-old waitress, Barbara Stoppel, is murdered while working at the Ideal Donut shop in Winnipeg.

1986: Charges against four men are laid in the Helen Betty Osborne case, 15 years after her murder. The following year, one of the four men arrested is convicted and sentenced to life in prison.

At trial, a jury failed to reach a unanimous verdict and a mistrial was declared on November 6, 1982. Twice more, Sophonow was tried for the murder. Even though these trials resulted in convictions, the verdicts were overthrown on appeal on the grounds that the judge had not adequately allowed the jury to consider the defense's arguments. At that point, the Court of Appeal agreed that while there were still grounds for a new trial, it refused to put Sophonow through a fourth ordeal. Sophonow had already served almost four years in prison for a crime he had consistently maintained that he did not commit.

Although the guilty verdict was set aside and he was acquitted, what Sophonow really wanted was exoneration. It was not until 1998 that the Winnipeg Police Service finally undertook a reinvestigation of the Barbara Stoppel murder. Two years later, the Attorney General apologized for Sophonow's treatment and declared him innocent of the murder.

The investigation also resulted in a public inquiry which produced 23 recommendations, including a revision of the use of in-custody informants and the awarding of $2.6 million in compensation to the wrongly convicted man.

1988: J. J. Harper, a young Native man, is killed by a Winnipeg police officer when he is mistaken for another person of Aboriginal descent. Public outcry leads to the launch of the Aboriginal Justice Inquiry.

1988: Christine Jack, the wife of a Winnipeg Blue Bombers football player, goes missing. Her husband Brian is accused of the crime but not convicted.

1991: James Driskell is sentenced for the 1991 murder of fellow thief Perry Harder in Winnipeg. The prosecution argued that Driskell killed Harder to prevent his testifying against him.

1999: The provincial government establishes the Aboriginal Justice Implementation Commission to recommend action on the Aboriginal Justice Inquiry's 1991 report.

Did you know...

that according to a city of Winnipeg by-law, the fine for a "cat running at large" is $100? Dog defecation results in a $200 penalty, while "owning or harbouring an unlicensed Pitbull" will set you back $1,500.

2000: Thomas Sophonow is exonerated in the Barbara Stoppel murder case. The Manitoba Department of Justice orders a Commission of Inquiry.

2003: Bank robber and former Winnipeg city official Klaus Burlakow, the "Fat Bandit," is apprehended after a high-speed chase on the outskirts of Winnipeg.

2003: James Driskell is released on bail after DNA evidence establishes that the three hairs found in his truck did not belong to Perry Harder, as had been claimed by the Crown.

2006: Manitoba Justice launches an inquiry into the wrongful conviction of James Driskell. The report was released to the public in 2007.

Winnipeg Policing Scandals

Manitoba's first police scandal was in 1875 when Winnipeg's initial Chief of Police, John S. Ingram, was arrested for frequenting a house of ill-repute. Fast forward to 1929 when Constable Jules Drapeau accused police chief Thomas Gagnon of diverting liquor destined for the St. Norbert Orphanage to bootlegger Jules Mourant. An investigation determined that Chief Gagnon was guilty not only of the liquor theft, but also of defrauding the Police Commission of government money paid to house destitute men staying overnight at the police station.

Since then, there have been numerous corruption incidents in the Winnipeg police force. The most heinous of these occurred in 1981 with the brutal murder of Paul Clear by his brother-in-law Barry Neilson and his accomplice Jerry Stolar, both police officers. The officers were part of a ring of cops involved in breaking and entering, and killed Clear in order to prevent him from turning them in.

Take 5   FIVE COLD CASES

1. **Christine Jack.** The wife of a Winnipeg Blue Bombers football player, she was last seen on December 17, 1988 and is widely believed to have been murdered. Her husband Brian was accused of the crime but his conviction did not withstand appeals. The body has never been found.

2. **Janice Howe.** The pretty 35-year-old left her parent's house in Winnipeg on the night of Friday, August 28, 1992. She was never seen again. She was driving her father's 1985 Oldsmobile Cierra, which turned up, empty, the next morning 19 miles east of Kenora, ON. Police suspect foul play, but cannot find her body to prove it.

3. **Barbara Stoppel.** On December 23, 1981, the vivacious 16-year-old was strangled to death while working as a waitress in a Winnipeg donut shop. Thomas Sophonow was wrongly convicted for the crime, but later exonerated. The true perpetrator has never been found.

4. **Mary Passage.** The 73-year-old ran "Aunt Mary's Tearoom," an establishment known for selling liquor after hours. In 1964, she was stabbed to death in the jugular and heart. The unsolved case drew attention to a chronic bootlegging problem in inner city Winnipeg during the 1960s.

5. **Julia Johnson.** On a spring afternoon in 1928, neighbours saw the five-year old playing with a tennis ball outside her house; minutes later she was gone. Although newspapers and the police offered a $2,000 reward, no one came forward. Nine years later, a machinist found a tiny mummified body and a tennis ball in the combustion chamber of a boiler in a nearby abandoned building under renovation. It was Julia. It was never established how the girl came to be there.
Source: Winnipeg Police.

2008: The Winnipeg Parking Authority announces big hikes in parking costs and fines. Mayor Sam Katz says currently Winnipeg is "the cheapest parking in Canada."

CRIME IN MANITOBA

Manitoba continues to have one of the highest crime rates in the country, with a rate of 11,678 per 100,000 population in 2006, second only to Saskatchewan's 13,711. The national crime rate was 7,518 in 2006, with Ontario recording the lowest provincial crime rate at 5,689.

Source: Statistics Canada.

CRIME BY THE NUMBERS (2006)

- 137,545 criminal code incidents
- 39 homicides
- 14,640 assaults
- 2,148 robberies
- 16,202 motor vehicle thefts
- 12,650 break and enters
- 1,273 sexual assaults
- 2,153 drug violations
- 2,506 cases of impaired driving
- 32,755 mischief cases

Did you know...

that since 1984, Winnipeg Crime Stoppers has received nearly 100,000 telephone tips? Winnipeg Crime Stoppers ranks fifth in North America in recovered property, including over 4,000 stolen vehicles.

Aboriginal Injustice

Aboriginal people in Manitoba have a long history of suffering at the hands of the justice system. A notable example occurred on March 9, 1988 when J.J. Harper was stopped by police who were looking for an Aboriginal male fleeing the scene of a car theft in downtown Winnipeg. Not realizing they had the wrong man, the officers confronted the young Aboriginal leader. During the ensuing scuffle, a shot was fired and Harper was killed.

A police investigation ruled the shooting an accident. The public was outraged, prompting Manitoba's NDP government to set up an Aboriginal Justice Inquiry. After concluding that Constable Robert Cross used excessive force during the confrontation, the inquiry expanded its mandate to other cases involving members of Manitoba's First Nations.

For two years, a panel traveled the province collecting testimony of Aboriginal people's experience with the justice system. One story that stood out was that of Helen Betty Osborne, who had dreamed of becoming a teacher in her community. Osborne left her home in Norway House, Manitoba to study in the nearby town of The Pas.

On the evening of November 13, 1971, while walking down Third Street, the 19-year-old was pulled into a car by four men. For hours they brutally beat and assaulted her, stabbing her at least 50 times with a screwdriver.

Despite her horrifically violent death, no one was charged. Ignoring reports that placed four drunken white men on the street that night, the police limited their interrogations to Osborne's Aboriginal friends.

It was not until 1986 that the case was finally reopened and arrests made. During the trial, it became evident that cruising the streets for sex with Aboriginal women was a common practice for white males in 1970s The Pas. Dwayne Johnston was ultimately convicted and sentenced to life in prison, but his accomplices never saw the inside of a cell.

It was situations like these that resulted in the Aboriginal Justice Inquiry's 150 recommendations for improving the provincial justice system. Although very few of these guidelines have ever been implemented, the process did eventually bring about a number of changes in the attitudes and procedures of the Winnipeg Police.

POLICING MANITOBA (2007)

- Number of police officers employed in Canada: 64,134
- Number of police officers employed in Manitoba: 2,409
- Number of Manitoba residents per officer: 491.0 (Canada: 512.3)
- Number of men employed: 2,026
- Number of women employed: 383
- Per capita expenditure on policing: $222 (Canada: $303)
- Number of emergency calls made to Winnipeg police: 196,189
- Number of red light cameras in Winnipeg: 48
- Number of police stations and service centres: 13

Sources: Statistics Canada, Winnipeg Police, Government of Manitoba.

CSI: MANITOBA

In 2006, the Forensic Services Unit in Winnipeg fingerprinted 13,898 individuals and processed 3,233 latent fingerprints, producing 822 positive fingerprint identifications. The unit also collected 436 DNA samples resulting in 43 suspects being identified in crimes, and conducted 89 technological crime investigations by retrieving and analyzing evidence from computers, cell phones and other electronic devices. Still, good old-fashioned pencil and paper has not gone out of style: 30 composite drawings were completed in 2006, producing 10 arrests.

Source: Winnipeg Police Annual Report.

Did you know...

that in 1998, the government of Manitoba built a high security $3.5 million courthouse specifically designed to try 35 gang members under a new federal law making it illegal to belong to a criminal organization? Most of the accused pleaded out to lesser offences, and the anti-gang charges were eventually dropped.

STOLEN CARS

Winnipeg enjoys the dubious distinction of being Canada's car theft capital. In 2006, there were 1,932 vehicles stolen for every 100,000 people, almost twice the 1,155 rate of second ranked Abbotsford, British Columbia. Toronto had a rate of only 294, the second lowest

Take 5 JACK TEMPLEMAN'S FIVE
MEMORABLE EVENTS IN MANITOBA POLICING

Jack Templeman retired from the Winnipeg Police Service after 35 years with the St. Boniface and Winnipeg departments. He was essential in organizing the Winnipeg Police Museum, and became its Curator/Historian after his 1994 retirement from active duty. He still holds that position.

1. **John Krafchenko** was a bank robber who killed the manager of the bank in Plum Coulee in 1913 and fled to Winnipeg. He was arrested and detained in the Rupert Station, but escaped with the aid of a crooked lawyer and a police jailer. The City and Provincial governments posted a reward of $10,000 for his capture, which was equal to about 10 years of an average person's wages. Krafchenko was caught, convicted and executed. The lawyer got three years in prison and was later reinstated to the Bar. The policeman was sentenced to seven years, and was killed in Stony Mountain Penitentiary.

2. **Earl Nelson**, known as "the Strangler," hitchhiked to Winnipeg in the 1920s and terrorized the city when he killed a young girl and then a married lady. He fled to Saskatchewan, but returned to Manitoba and hitchhiked toward the US border. He was spotted south of Killarney and arrested by Manitoba Provincial Police. He was positively identified as being a roomer in homes where 24 US murders took place, and was also ID'd in connection with the two Winnipeg killings. Nelson was the last man executed at the Vaughan Street Jail in downtown Winnipeg in 1928.

(after Quebec City) for an urban centre with a population over 500,000.

The car theft rate for the province of Manitoba was 1,376, almost double that of number two Alberta's 725, and nearly three times the Canadian average of 487 motor vehicle thefts per 100,000 people.

3. **Michael Vescio** was a soldier who was also a sex pervert in the mid 1940s. He attacked a number of young boys and murdered two of them. The entire city was in a state of terror and young boys did not go out alone. He was finally arrested because the Winnipeg Police used a mine detector for the first time in North America to locate the bullets which were matched to an army gun that Vescio had stolen and was caught with during a robbery.

4. **The Winnipeg General Strike Action** in 1919 saw the Winnipeg Police form an unauthorized union. Advised to get out or be fired, 228 refused to leave the union and were fired. Only 23 remained on the job. The streets were patrolled by up to 1,400 "Special Constables" for about six weeks before regular police were rehired.

5. **John Ingram**, Winnipeg's first Chief Constable, served for only one year between 1874 and 1875. A booming metropolis, Winnipeg was known as a wicked city because of its drinking establishments and red-light districts. The Chief had a weakness for women and frequented a house of ill-fame which upset two constables who did not get along with him. When they searched a known house of prostitution on Sherbrooke Street, they found Chief Constable Ingram "in a state of undress" and promptly arrested him. He was convicted, fined $8.00, and forced to resign.

NUMBER OF VEHICLES STOLEN IN MANITOBA

- 1995: 7,887
- 2005: 11,736
- 2006: 16,202

Sources: Winnipeg Police Service, Statistics Canada, Institute of Chartered Accountants of Manitoba CBC, Winnipeg Free Press.

IMPAIRED DRIVING

In 2006, Manitoba's impaired driving rate per 100,000 was 212.8, just below the national average of 227.9, and less than half Saskatchewan's rate of 473.8, the highest in the country. Ontario has the most cars of any province, but recorded the lowest rate of impaired driving with 139.1.

In 2005/2006, 1,217 people were charged with impaired driving in Manitoba; of those, only 5.3 percent were incarcerated as a result. In 2006, 98 people were killed in motor vehicle accidents; nearly half of those deaths involved alcohol.

Source: Statistics Canada, CBC.

Did you know...

that among Canadian census metro areas of over 500,000 people, Winnipeg has the highest rate of police officers per 100,000 population with 188? Montreal and Toronto are second and third with 184 and 175 respectively.

FINE, THEN

Parking in a no-parking zone	$35
Driving with an obscured plate	$92
Speeding	From $144 (10-12 km over limit) to $1,074 (100-120 km over limit)
Running a red light	$167
Failure to wear a seatbelt	$247
Operating a snowmobile without a permit	$247
Driving without insurance	$557
Passing a stopped school bus	$557

Source: Manitoba Justice.

The Double Life of Klaus Burlakow

City official cum bank robber, Klaus Burlakow led a complicated double life until he was arrested in 2003. A senior manager with the City of Winnipeg, the bureaucrat was responsible for event planning, including the successful realization of the 1999 Pan-American Games, a royal visit, and Mayor Glen Murray's first downtown street party in July 2001.

Seemingly, this was not excitement enough. After leaving his $123,000 a year job, Burlakow divided his time between Winnipeg and Seattle where he assumed an alternate identity as a millionaire Irish war hero named Patrick Burke. Beguiled by his soft-spoken charm, a local woman entered into a business and romantic relationship with the duplicitous entrepreneur. Burlakow's unsuspecting wife remained in Winnipeg while her husband rented luxury cars and stayed in Seattle's best hotels.

Unable to support his expensive double life, the 47-year-old donned a disguise and embraced yet another secret identity, this time as a bank robber. Between November 2002 and February 2003, in broad daylight, Burlakow robbed six banks in Winnipeg, one in Vancouver and another in Seattle. Dubbed the "Fat Bandit" by local police, he was eventually caught after a high speed chase in Winnipeg's outskirts. Burlakow was sentenced to eight years in prison.

They Said It

YOUTH CRIME RATE

Youth charged with a criminal offence (per 100,000)

- Manitoba: 5,446.7
- Canada: 3,327

Source: Statistics Canada.

DOING TIME

A third of the 10,444 people convicted of crimes in Manitoba in 2005/2006 served time. In addition to the 3,452 people who went to prison, 355 or 3 percent received conditional sentences, and 2,002 or 19 percent were placed on probation. Another 2,453 or 23 percent paid fines, while 2,147 of those convicted received a variety of other punishments, including suspended sentences, community service and prohibition orders, among others. A few miscreants convicted late in 2006 were not sentenced until 2007.

Did you know...

that in 2004 Manitoba became the fourth province to legalize same-sex marriage?

Did you know...

that the fine for unauthorized burning of crop stubble between August 1 and November 15 is $2,107?

HANGING OUT AT THE VAUGHAN STREET JAIL

Between 1874 and 1952, 52 people were executed in Manitoba. Of those, 35 were hanged at Winnipeg's Vaughan Street Jail. Built in 1881 to house both male and female offenders, the jail saw its initial hanging in 1899 with the execution of Manitoba's first mass murderers, Wazyl Guszczak and Simeon Czubej by professional hangman John Radclive.

After 1930, Manitoba's gallows moved to the newly opened Headingley prison complex just west of Winnipeg. The last man executed in the province was Henry Malanik who met his fate in June 1952, 24 years before capital punishment was officially banned in Canada.

Riot in Headingley

The Headingley Correctional Institution has been rife with violence ever since its October 1930 opening. In its first decade there were four inmate revolts, and then one in each subsequent decade.

The institution's most serious riots broke out at 11:00 pm on April 25, 1996 and continued for 24 hours. During this time the prison was the scene of fires and brutal attacks on guards and inmates. Three hundred twenty-one prisoners eventually surrendered, and eight guards and 17 inmates were treated for injuries. Although no one was killed, one prisoner lost fingers and another was nearly castrated. The Headingley jail was reduced to a burned-out shell in the wake of the riot, and it took more than a year for it to be rebuilt.

Some attributed it to the riot on the policy of encouraging guards to act as social workers. Others blamed gang wars, staff cuts and policy changes that allowed high security inmates to come in contact with the general prison population. An investigation revealed that targeted inmates were either informants, or had been segregated because of sex crimes.

Take 5 **FIVE UNUSUAL**
FINEABLE OFFENCES

1. Leaving a shopping cart unattended ($167)
2. Driving an unclean livestock truck on the highway ($144)
3. As a pedestrian, walking more than two abreast ($92)
4. Riding on a part of a bicycle not designed for passengers ($92)
5. Operating an improperly installed TV set while driving ($92)

Source: Government of Manitoba.

CORRECTIONAL FACILITIES
Federal Centres:

Stony Mountain	medium security	546 adult males

Provincial Centres:

Brandon	medium security	157 adult males
Dauphin	minimum	50 adult males
Headingley	min/med/max	458 adult males
Portage	min/med	45 adult females
The Pas	medium	70 adult males/ 7 adult females
Milner Ridge	minimum	115 adult males
Winnipeg Remand	pre-trial/min/ med/max	289 males & females
Agassiz	youth facility	variable number of males & females
Manitoba Youth	youth facility	157 young males & females

Source: Government of Manitoba.

They Said It

"The arrangements in the jail were splendid; it is seldom I see anything so well arranged. There was none of the usual crowding and my task was comparatively easy. If all sheriffs and governors were as careful and thoughtful as yours in Winnipeg, things would be all right, and the executioner would have nothing to complain about. As for the hanging, the men never moved after the drop and I consider the work a success."

**– John Radclive, Canada's "executioner of choice,"
following his 1899 visit to Winnipeg's Vaughan Street Jail.**

Weblinks

Winnipeg Police Service
http://www.winnipeg.ca/police/
Everything you need to know about crime in the capital, from prevention to the latest news. The excellent history and museum section is chock full of exciting stories about crime in Manitoba.

Crime Stoppers
http://www.manitobacrimestoppers.com/index.html
Stay current on the latest unsolved crimes; links to the Winnipeg and Brandon sites.

Manitoba Justice
http://www.gov.mb.ca/justice/
Information on topics including domestic violence and stalking, as well as developing safer communities and employment opportunities.

Culture

Long before the word "multicultural" came into the lingo, Manitoba was a diverse society in which First Nations, French and Anglo cultures alternately battled one another, mixed, and co-existed. In the late 1800s and early 20th century, European immigrants, notably Russian Jews, Icelanders, Germans and Ukrainians brought their traditions to the province. Since the 1960s, Manitoba has become truly international, and now boasts residents from countries around the globe.

Manitoba's cultural origins are very much alive today. Winnipeg is known as the Aboriginal Capital of Canada, with more First Nations peoples living in the Manitoba capital than any other major city in the country. Winnipeg also has one of Canada's largest French speaking populations outside of Quebec.

Folkorama, a two-week long festival held every August, highlights the food, culture and music of over 40 nationalities and ethnicities, and provides an ideal opportunity to discover Manitoba's rich cultural mosaic.

Manitoba's isolated location has produced a vibrant artistic and cultural scene. Winnipeg is home to the world-renowned Royal Winnipeg Ballet, the Winnipeg Symphony Orchestra, the Rainbow Stage Theatre, the Winnipeg Folk Festival, the Winnipeg Art Gallery and the Manitoba Museum.

Manitoba's culture comes in many forms, from the province's award-winning authors, to the Salisbury House restaurant chain, to

Winnipeg Blue Bombers football. Still, whether it's "high" culture, "low" culture, or something in between, all of it bears the unmistakable stamp of diverse, creative and ingenious people.

ARTISTS
- Number of artists in Canada: 130,695
- Number of artists in Manitoba: 4,000
- Percentage of those who live in Winnipeg: 74

WINNIPEG HAS
- 120 actors
- 380 artisans and craftpersons
- 60 conductors, composers and arrangers
- 245 dancers
- 1,045 musicians and singers
- 110 other performers
- 280 painters, sculptors, and other visual artists
- 300 producers, directors, choreographers and related
- 430 writers

CULTURAL SPENDING
- Manitobans spent $850 million on cultural goods and services in 2005, which was the fifth highest in the country at $809 per person.
- Manitoba ranks third in the country in per capita funding from the Canada Council for the Arts.
- Manitobans spent an average of $257 on books and other printed matter in 2006, just below the Canadian average of $264.

THAT'S AN ORDER
- Manitoba recipients of the Order of Canada: 223
- Members of the Order: 163
- Officers of the Order: 51
- Companions of the Order: 9

ORDER OF MANITOBA

The Order of Manitoba was established in 1999 by then Lieutenant Governor Peter M. Liba and is the highest honour in the province. It is awarded annually to approximately 12 people who have made an outstanding contribution to the province in the areas of culture, business or public service. To date, there have been 109 individuals called to the Order of Manitoba — about 25 percent of who are from the cultural sector.

Take 5 — GUY MADDIN'S TOP FIVE
GHOST STRUCTURES IN WINNIPEG

Known for his original style and offbeat humour, Winnipeg filmmaker Guy Maddin has directed nine feature films and several shorts, many of them shot in or around Winnipeg. Several of his films have local cult status including *The Saddest Music in the World*, *Brand Upon the Brain!* and *My Winnipeg*, which has been described as a "docu-fantasia."

1. **Winnipeg Arena on Maroons Road**. The hockey shrine was torn down in 2006, and was the home of the ghostly Winnipeg Jets and the great, long-buried Canadian national teams of the 60s. It hosted game three of the legendary 1972 Summit Series.
2. **Clifford's Clothing Store**, currently Hakeem Optical on Portage Avenue. This building, with its retro-style and floors of women's fashions during the '70s, was once a downtown landmark.
3. **Lyceum Theatre**, a fantastic grindhouse, was torn down in the '60s to make way for what is now the Radisson.
4. **Chelsea Court**, at the corner of Kennedy Street and Assiniboine Avenue, was our own Chateau Marmont and was recently allowed to die of neglect. The charm and character of these 1914 riverside apartments and courtyards was not enough to save them.
5. **Metropolitan Theatre**, vacated for 20 years, lives out a zombie existence opposite our new zombie arena in the zombie-haunted downtown of Winnipeg.

ART

The Winnipeg Art Gallery (WAG) was founded in 1912, and is western Canada's oldest public art gallery. It is home to the world's largest collection of contemporary Inuit art. WAG shows work by regional, national and international artists, and frequently hosts readings, lectures, live music and educational programs.

FILM INDUSTRY

Manitoba's film industry is booming, with production budgets increasing from a meager $500,000 in 1986, to $114 million in 2006-2007. Most of the big name film shoots have taken place in Winnipeg's Exchange District, a well-preserved grouping of early 20th century buildings in the heart of the city. But slowly, filmmakers are hearing about the charms of Manitoba small towns, and film shoots have occurred in numerous rural locations including Birds Hill Provincial Park, Selkirk, Emerson and Hartney.

Did you know...

that Neil Young spent his teenage years in Winnipeg? Young and his mother moved to the city from Toronto after his parents divorced. While in Winnipeg, Young attended Kelvin High School and played in several local bands, notably the Squires, before heading to Toronto and ultimately California.

FIVE SPECIALIZED
THEATRE GROUPS IN MANITOBA

1. **Manitoba Theatre for Young People**. Year-round live theatre for kids, known by the locals as MTYP. Located at the Forks.
2. **Le Cercle Molière**. Year-round St. Boniface venue specializing in French Canadian performances.
3. **Rainbow Stage**. Outdoor productions under the canopy in Winnipeg's Kildonan Park. Held each summer.
4. **Manitoba's Passion Play**. The story of Christ, performed live each summer near La Riviere.
5. **MTC's Warehouse Theatre**. Just around the corner from the Manitoba Theatre Centre's Main Stage, it offers great alternative theatre that's occasionally way out in left field.

LIVE THEATRE

Live theatre is huge in Manitoba. And there's a theatrical group to appeal to pretty much every demographic. The primary venue for live traditional and contemporary theatre is the main stage of the Manitoba Theatre Centre (MTC), a Winnipeg-based community-run company that has just completed its 50th year.

Did you know...

that master bronze sculptor Leo Mol's commissioned and gallery pieces are exhibited around the world? Mol, an Officer of the Order of Canada, was born in the Ukraine in 1915 and moved to Winnipeg in 1948. More than 200 pieces of his work are displayed in the Leo Mol Sculpture Garden at Assiniboine Park in Winnipeg.

Did you know...

that Winnipeg's 180,000-square foot Millennium Library, which opened in 2005, took two years to complete and cost $18,000,000?

MUSIC

A number of rock legends got their start in Winnipeg bars and clubs back in the 1960s, including Neil Young and The Guess Who. Winnipeg still has a vibrant music scene, with at least half a dozen excellent concert venues, and numerous bars and festivals where you can catch great live music at reasonable prices.

Bachman &Cummings-Canada's Answer to Lennon and McCartney

Winnipeggers Randy Bachman and Burton Cummings came together over forty years ago as members of The Guess Who. The two split for some time, but have reunited as the duo Bachman Cummings, and are once again touring and recording together; their most recent album is *Jukebox* (2007). Bachman and Cummings have both been called to the Order of Manitoba (independently), and received the Governor General's Performing Arts Award as members of The Guess Who.

The Guess Who, which evolved from Chad Allan and the Expressions, was formed in 1962 and is among rock's most enduring acts. Bachman was an original member, while Cummings joined in 1966 when Allan left the band. The Guess Who scored a hit with the cover "Shakin' All Over" in 1965, but really made the big time in 1968 when they released the Bachman/Cummings penned smash, "These Eyes." Other hits followed, including "Laughing," "No Time" and "American Woman," which was made popular again in 1999 by American rocker Lenny Kravitz.

The good times for the band didn't last. In 1970, Bachman, a Mormon, left The Guess Who in opposition to the group's wild lifestyle. He soon formed Bachman-Turner Overdrive; a number of

DANCE

The Royal Winnipeg Ballet (RWB) is one of the world's most famous dance troupes. Founded in 1939, it is the longest continuously operating ballet company in North America. The RWB established itself on the international stage under the leadership of Arnold Spohr, who was its artistic director from 1958 to 1988. The RWB spends about twenty weeks of the year on the road, and it was the first western company to

the band's songs, including "Takin' Care of Business," and "You Ain't Seen Nothing Yet," remain classic rock staples.

In addition to his work with Bachman Turner Overdrive, the versatile Bachman fronted the band Ironhorse, and has also recorded a number of solo albums, some of them in a jazz and country vein. Bachman, who was born in 1943 in Winnipeg, now lives on Salt Spring Island, BC, and hosts a syndicated radio program called "Randy's Vinyl Tap" that airs on CBC radio on Saturday nights.

For his part, Burton Cummings left The Guess Who in the mid 1970s, and has since recorded five solo albums, scoring a million selling single in 1976 with "Stand Tall." He has also dabbled in movies, co-starring in the movie, *Melanie* in 1982. Cummings, who was born on New Year's Eve 1947, spends winters in California, and the rest of the year at his home in Winnipeg where he is part owner of the Salisbury House restaurant chain. In 2002, Winnipeg's 1,646-seat Walker Theatre (which was built in 1907) was renamed the Burton Cummings Theatre for the Performing Arts.

Like their British counterparts Lennon and McCartney, you can't argue with the success of either Bachman or Cummings on their own, but you also have to think that as a pair they are even better.

appear in post-Revolution Cuba. All told, the CWB has performed in 573 cities worldwide. Under the direction of current Artistic Director André Lewis, the RWB is as vibrant as ever, commissioning new versions of *The Magic Flute*, *The Nutcracker* and *Dracula*. In addition to

Speed Skater Cindy Klassen

Cindy Klassen is fast. World record-breaking fast — Olympic gold fast! Yes, at the 2006 Winter Olympics in Turin, Italy, Cindy became the first Canadian Olympian to win five medals (one gold, two silver and two bronze) in one Olympic Games and the only Canadian with six Olympic medals to her credit (she also won a bronze in the 2002 Olympics in Salt Lake City). Despite her success, Klassen's first love wasn't competitive skating, it was hockey.

It all started when Cindy was two years old. Her father had made her a tiny wooden stick, and played street hockey with her every day in front of their Winnipeg home. Cindy played hockey on boys' teams, eventually switching to a girls' team at age 16. But a career in hockey was not to be — Cindy was not chosen for the 1998 Olympic women's hockey team as she had dreamed.

Undaunted, Klassen turned her focus to speed skating, and began winning championships. In 2003, Cindy became the first Canadian woman to win the World Championship Cup in 27 years, receiving the designation the "Best Allround Speed Skater in the World for 2003."

Klassen has capitalized on her athletic prowess. In 2006, she signed the most lucrative endorsement deal ever for an amateur athlete in Canada when she accepted a sponsorship agreement with Manitoba communications giant MTS. Klassen has been appearing in light-hearted commercials with the MTS bison mascot ever since.

In July 2006 Cindy was called to the Order of Manitoba, and in December 2006 she received the Lou Marsh Trophy, an award given to the Canadian Athlete of the Year.

Did you know...

that in 1974 Terry Jacks hit #1 on the Canadian, US and the UK pop charts with the song "Seasons in the Sun"? The single has sold over 11 million copies. Jacks was born in Winnipeg in 1944, and has lived in British Columbia since the 1960s. Today, Jacks, who has also produced many albums for other artists, is best known for his environmental activism.

the RWB, Winnipeg is home to two contemporary dance companies, a school of contemporary dance, and the Bolero Dance Theatre (a company specializing in Spanish dance).

JUNO AWARDS

Since the Juno Awards were established in 1971, Manitoba artists have received a total of 205 nominations and 53 awards, including seven Aboriginal music awards. Winnipeg hosted the Juno Awards in 2005; the event was held at the MTS Center and the Tragically Hip were inducted into the Canadian Music Hall of Fame. Native sons Randy Bachman and Burton Cummings performed; however, Neil Young, who had been scheduled to appear, had to bow out as he was recovering from a brain aneurysm.

Did you know...

that Winnipeg-born David Steinberg, one of television's leading comic directors, writers and producers, ranks second only to Bob Hope in *Tonight Show* appearances? Steinberg was born in 1942, grew up in Winnipeg's North End and was a popular 1960s standup comic. In addition to the *Tonight Show*, Steinberg was an important part of *The Smothers Brothers Comedy Hour,* and in the 1970s hosted *The David Steinberg Show*, which featured future SCTV stars John Candy, Martin Short, Joe Flaherty, Dave Thomas and Andrea Martin.

CULINARY OPTIONS

Manitoba has a cornucopia of restaurants, with more than 1,100 eateries in Winnipeg alone. Other Manitoba delights include Salisbury House "Nips" (hamburgers served with fried onions), coarse ham/garlic sausage (buy it at a butcher shop or grocery store), Ukrainian perogies and smoked Goldeye.

Take 5 TOP FIVE MANITOBA NOVELISTS

1. **Gabrielle Roy** (1909-1983) was born and raised in St. Boniface and taught school there for seven years. She left Manitoba for Europe, and ultimately settled in Quebec. A three-time Governor-General's Annual Literary Award winner, Roy wrote in French and is author of the *Tin Flute* and other CanLit classics.

2. **Margaret Laurence** (1926-1987) was born in Neepawa and attended Winnipeg's United College. Laurence would go on to live in England, Africa, British Columbia and Ontario, but the small-town prairies of her youth was often the setting for her novels which included *A Jest of God, The Stone Angel* and *The Diviners*.

3. **Carol Shields** (1935-2003), like Ernest Hemingway, was born in Oak Park, Illinois. She moved to Winnipeg in 1980, and wrote a number of books including *The Republic of Love* and *The Stone Diaries*, winner of the 1993 Governor General's Award and the Pulitzer Prize.

4. **Tomson Highway** (1951-). Highway, a Cree, was born in a tent in northern Manitoba and from the age of six raised in a residential school in The Pas. He was trained as a musician, but is best known as a playwright who has explored Aboriginal and gay themes in his writing. Highway is also author of two novels and several children's books.

5. **David Bergen** (1957-). Bergen, like fellow Manitoba writers Armin Wiebe and Miriam Toews, is a Mennonite. He moved from British Columbia to the small town of Niverville, Manitoba when he was an adolescent. Bergen now lives in Winnipeg and is the author of several acclaimed novels including *The Time in Between* (2005), which is influenced by the time he spent living in Vietnam.

Take 5   FIVE SONGS ABOUT MANITOBA

1. **"Moody Manitoba Morning"** (written by Rick Neufeld; recorded in 1969 by The Bells).
2. **"Prairie Town"** (written and performed by Randy Bachman, from the 1993 album *Any Road*).
3. **"Prairie Wind"** (written and performed by Neil Young from the 2005 album *Prairie Wind*).
4. **"Trains of Winnipeg"** (written and performed by Clive Holden, from the 2001 CD of the same name; part of a multi-media *Trains of Winnipeg* project that includes short films and a book).
5. **"One Great City"** (written and performed by The Weakerthans, from their 2003 *Reconstruction Site* CD).

MANITOBANS LOVE THEIR COFFEE

It's a Manitoba fact that you can't drive by a Tim Horton's without seeing a line-up at the drive-thru. There are 63 Tim Horton's (located in nine different municipalities) in the province. US import Starbuck's is popular too, with 19 stores. Add Second Cup franchises, and locally owned operations like Winnipeg's Black Pearl Coffee Roasters to the pot, and that's a lot of caffeine that Manitobans are swilling.

DRINK UP!

Fort Garry Brewing Company is king of Manitoba craft beers. Established in 1908, Fort Garry was sold to Molson's in 1960, but was resurrected in 1990 by Richard Hoeschen, a descendant of the brewery's founders. In 2003, Fort Garry amalgamated with another local operation, Twin River Brewery. Fort Garry offers nine different brews, including the high octane Stone Cold, which comes in a two-litre jug.

If wine is more to your liking, Winnipeg-based D.D. Leobard makes a tasty line-up of award-winning fruit wines and fruit dessert wines, while Rigby Orchards of Killarney specializes in berry wines.

SPORTS

Manitobans are passionate about sports, both as participants and spectators, and Winnipeg hosted the Pan American Games in 1967 and 1999.

Because of its long, cold winters, you'll be hard-pressed to find a Manitoba town that does not have a curling rink to help the locals pass away the dark months between November and March. There are dozens of rinks scattered throughout the province, and curling is the number one participatory sport in Manitoba.

And some people get pretty good at it! The Jennifer Jones team from Manitoba beat Alberta in February at the 2008 Scotties Tournament of Hearts in Regina. The victory gave the team the honour of representing Canada at the 2008 World Women's Curling Championships, which they proceeded to win.

The Weakerthans:
Winnipeg's Punk Folkies

Just in case you were thinking that all of Manitoba's rock icons are from long ago, think again. The Weakerthans, a favourite band of former Winnipeg mayor Glen Murray, are one of Canada's top indie acts.

Founding member John K. Samson started the eclectic Winnipeg band in 1997, and his introspective song writing, distinctive vocals and lead guitar are the band's signature stamp. Samson is married to fellow Manitoba-born musician Christine Fellows, and the two frequently collaborate on musical projects.

The quirky band is not easy to categorize, and the labels "folk," "alt-country," "punk," "alternative," and various combinations of the preceding have been applied to their music. One thing is for sure, the band is rooted in Manitoba; the song "One Great City" with its "I Hate Winnipeg" closing line is something only locals could get away with.

They Said It

> "*Every professional athlete owes a debt of gratitude to the fans and management, and pays an installment every time he plays. He should never miss a payment.*"
> – **The Winnipeg Jets' Bobby Hull, the first million-dollar hockey player.**

Skating is big in the province, too. Public skating is popular throughout the winter on the rivers at the Forks. Known as the "River Trail," this 8.5 km Winnipeg skateway is the longest in the country. In February 2008, a world record was set when 1,438 people formed a human chain and skated the trail for five minutes.

For those who like to get on the fast track, speed skating is also popular, and Manitoba has produced some of the best speed skaters in the world — notably Olympic medalists Clara Hughes and Cindy Klassen.

Take 5 MANITOBA'S TOP FIVE
MUSIC FESTIVALS

1. **Winnipeg Folk Festival** (folk, grass roots and world music; held each July at Birds Hill Provincial Park).
2. **Dauphin Countryfest** (Canada's longest running country fest, held at an outdoor venue in Dauphin on or near the July long weekend).
3. **Manito Ahbee Music Fest** (part of the 10-day Manito Ahbee First Nations festival held each fall at various venues around Winnipeg).
4. **Jazz Winnipeg Festival** (held each June).
5. **New Music Festival** (held by the Winnipeg Symphony Orchestra each winter, the festival celebrates the best from new composers).

Did you know...

that Winnipeg is one of the world's great places to see street art? There are 581 murals dotting city streets.

FOOTBALL

Established in 1930, the community-owned Winnipeg Blue Bombers were the first football team west of Ontario to capture the Grey Cup. Since that 1935 win, the Canadian Football League (CFL) team has captured the silver chalice nine more times. Winnipeg Stadium is home to the Bombers. University football is also big in Manitoba, and the University of Manitoba Bison won the Vanier Cup in 2007, per-

Take 5 — GAIL ASPER'S FIVE MOST CULTURALLY UNIQUE MANITOBA EXPERIENCES

Gail Asper is president of the CanWest Global Foundation, and is also president of The Asper Foundation, which is currently spearheading the creation of the Canadian Museum for Human Rights in Winnipeg. She serves and has served on the boards of numerous not-for-profit groups, and is currently co-chair of the Manitoba Theatre Centre Endowment Campaign, as well as vice-chair of the Council for Business and the Arts. Asper also serves on the board of directors for the National Arts Centre Foundation, is a director emeritus for the University of Waterloo Centre for Cultural Management and is Governor of the Hebrew University of Jerusalem. A lawyer by training, Gail Asper is corporate secretary of CanWest Global Communications, and has been called to the Order of Manitoba. She is married to Dr. Michael Paterson and has two children, Stephen and Jonathan.

1. **Manitoba Theatre Centre (MTC)** – now celebrating its 50th year, Canada's oldest English-speaking regional theatre provides the finest in the classics, musicals, and modern thought-provoking plays. Cutting edge productions are found at the MTC's Warehouse Theatre, and the MTC produced a 12-day cornucopia of theatre known as the Fringe Festival; a cultural jewel beyond compare!

They Said It

"The library card was my first official document as a citizen, and at the age of six I began to understand its power. It was a key and it opened the world."

– **Carol Shields, Order of Manitoba, award-winning author, 1935-2003.**

haps some consolation to Manitoba football fans who saw their beloved Bombers fall to their arch rivals, the Saskatchewan Rough Riders, in the 2007 Grey Cup.

2. **Royal Winnipeg Ballet** – is a world-class ballet company that is beloved around the world as well as in Winnipeg.

3. **The Manitoba Museum** – this is one of the top museums in Canada and is a place my kids loved to go on the weekends. Whether it was enjoying the "Touch the Universe" science exhibits, running around the *Nonsuch*, studying the artifacts from the Hudson's Bay collection or pretending they were living in a turn of the century village and watching silent Charlie Chaplin pictures, they always enjoyed themselves and never wanted to leave.

4. **The Winnipeg Folk Festival** – although there are folk festivals all around North America, the traditions of the Winnipeg Folk Festival make this truly unique, not to mention the spectacular prairie skies as the sun is setting.

5. **The Festival du Voyageur** – I always try to get out to see the fabulous snow sculptures that are an integral part of the festival. One of the great things about living in a colder city is that we can create the most amazing snow sculptures. I also love the sleigh rides, dog sled races, making maple syrup suckers and enjoying the performances at the festival site. I saw my first display of hoop dancing there and have never forgotten it!

Hockey

Manitobans are still smarting from the loss of their beloved Winnipeg Jets. Launched as a member of the World Hockey Association (WHA) in 1972, the Jets joined the National Hockey League (NHL) in 1979.

The WHA franchise got off to a bang with the signing of superstar Bobby Hull, the "Golden Jet," who jumped from the NHL Chicago Blackhawks to play in Winnipeg. While in Winnipeg, Hull was accompanied by a talented cast of Swedes; this at a time when there were almost no Europeans playing in North America.

The WHA party didn't last long, but the Jets made the most of it, winning three Avco Cups in the league's seven years of existence. The NHL Jets never won a Stanley Cup, but did make 11 playoff appearances and boasted stars including Dale Hawerchuk and Thomas Steen. The Jets' home, Winnipeg Arena, hosted Game Three of the 1972 Summit Series with the Soviet Union, and was the scene for many a "white-out" at play-off time when fans turned out dressed in white to cheer on their team.

In 1996, due to financial difficulties, Winnipeg's NHL franchise relocated to Phoenix and became the Coyotes. Popular as they were, the Jets were hardly the province's first high profile team. The Winnipeg Victorias won Stanley Cups in 1896, 1901 and 1902, and the Winnipeg Falcons, a squad initially formed of players of Icelandic origin who were denied the chance to play on other teams because of ethnic prejudice, won the Gold Medal at the 1920 Olympics in Antwerp, Belgium.

Today, hockey fans rally around the Manitoba Moose, a member of the American Hockey League (AHL) and the farm team for the Vancouver Canucks. Home ice for the Moose is Winnipeg's True North/MTS Centre. The Moose are captained by Winnipeg native Mike Keane, who strapped on the skates in 2008-09 for his 21st season of professional hockey. The other Manitoba team of note is the Brandon Wheat Kings of the Western Hockey League. The Junior team is consistently one of the best in the league, and includes among its alumni former and current NHLers Glen Hanlon, Brian Propp, Ron Hextall, Ray Ferraro and Jordin Tootoo.

BASEBALL

Named after the popular Lake Winnipeg fish, the Winnipeg Goldeyes swam their way into the hearts of Manitobans by winning the Northern League championship in 1994, their inaugural season. The "Fish" played in the Winnipeg Stadium for five years before the CanWest Global Stadium was built to house them in 1999. The franchise set the Northern League single season attendance mark in 2004, and holds the

Bio MIRIAM TOEWS

Miriam Toews was born in Steinbach in 1964 and has already won several major literary awards, including the Governor General's Award, the McNally Robinson Book of the Year, and the Margaret Laurence Award for Fiction.

Toews' first novel, *The Summer of My Amazing Luck*, was published in 1996. Since then, she has published *A Boy of Good Breeding* (fiction), *Swing Low: A life* (a memoir devoted to her father), and *A Complicated Kindness* — the novel for which she received the prestigious Governor General's Award. Toews' most recent novel is *The Flying Troutmans* which was released in the fall of 2008. Toews grew up in a conservative Mennonite environment, and much of her fiction, which is by turns moving and humorous, is rooted in the small town Manitoba of her youth.

Toews obtained a Film Studies degree from the University of Manitoba, and followed that up with a journalism degree from King's College in Halifax. Prior to embarking on fiction writing, she wrote articles for a number of publications, and also worked as freelance radio producer for the CBC. Recently, she has tried her hand at acting, appearing in the 2007 movie *Silent Light*. Toews lives in Winnipeg and has two children — Owen, born in 1987 and Georgia, born in 1990. "I love writing, but my main focus has always been raising my kids," says Miriam.

Take 5 TOP FIVE MANITOBA-BORN
NHL GREATS

1. **Andy Bathgate**, Center (NY Rangers, Toronto, Pittsburgh, Detroit), born 1932, Winnipeg.
2. **Terry Sawchuk**, Goaltender (Detroit, Toronto, Boston, NY Rangers, Los Angeles), born 1929, Winnipeg; died 1970.
3. **Bobby Clarke**, Center (Philadelphia) born 1949, Flin Flon.
4. **Ron Hextall**, Goaltender (Philadelphia, NY Islanders, Quebec) born 1964, Brandon.
5. **Ed Belfour**, Goaltender (Chicago, San Jose, Dallas, Toronto, Florida) born 1965, Carman.

record for longest Northern League game played. Goldeyes owner and president Sam Katz has a side gig as mayor of Winnipeg.

Take 5 FIVE GREAT VENUES
TO SEE LIVE MUSIC IN WINNIPEG

1. **Centennial Concert Hall.** Located in the heart of downtown, the elegant 2,300-seat venue is home to the Royal Winnipeg Ballet, the Winnipeg Symphony Orchestra and the Manitoba Opera Association.
2. **Pantages Playhouse Theatre.** Opened in 1914, the Pantages has played host to luminaries including Sir Laurence Olivier and Queen Elizabeth. The Pantages is located in the Exchange District National Historic Site.
3. **The Lyric Theatre.** The Assiniboine Park venue is a great spot for free outdoor summer concerts.
4. **West End Cultural Centre.** Established in 1987, the centre is a renovated church and is an intimate concert for folk, international and spoken word performers.
5. **MTS Centre.** A multi-purpose sports and entertainment centre which is home to the Manitoba Moose. Rush, Avril Lavigne, Kanye West, Mariah Carey, and Eric Clapton are just some of the acts who have played the MTS Centre in the last several years.

Weblinks

Winnipeg Public Library

http://www.millenniumlibrary.com

For information about hours, public literary events, to hook up with the local writer-in-residence, or to just be wowed by the fabulous architecture of the building.

Winnipeg Art Gallery

www.wag.mb.ca

For information about current exhibits and events.

Destination Winnipeg

www.destinationwinnipeg.ca

For a complete calendar of events in the big city.

Did you know...

that Winnipeg's Clara Hughes is the world's only athlete to win two or more medals in each of the Summer and Winter Olympic Games? She won a gold and silver in speed skating in 2006, as well as two bronze medals for cycling in 1996.

Did you know...

that Major League Baseball player Corey Koskie hails from Anola? Koskie was born in 1973 and graduated from Springfield Collegiate High School in Oakbank. He was drafted by the Minnesota Twins in 1994, and has played for Minnesota, Toronto and Milwaukee.

Economy

Manitoba's economy is in solid shape — unemployment and inflation are relatively low, GDP growth is steady, and the province has recently been posting surpluses after years of red ink. Manitoba wages lag those in a number of other provinces, particularly Ontario and Alberta; however, Manitoba's moderate cost of living generally makes up for the disparity. Moreover, Manitoba's recent economic resurgence follows decades of mediocre performance when many left the province in search of better opportunities elsewhere.

Prior to the establishment of Manitoba as a province in 1870, the fur trade was the dominant economic activity, and the Hudson's Bay Company was key in developing the region. Manitoba's economic base expanded in the late 1800s as waves of newcomers settled on farms, and Winnipeg developed into an important rail transportation center.

The boom times didn't last, however, as completion of the Panama Canal in 1914 (which lessened Winnipeg's role as an east-west transportation gateway), falling world grain prices and the Depression had a negative effect on the province's fortunes. Manitoba's economy did recover in the post WWII era, but the province was sharing in Canadian prosperity, rather than acting as an engine of it.

The last several years have seen a noticeable upturn, thanks to Manitoba's diverse economy in which the agriculture, transportation

They Said It

and natural resources areas are complemented by a robust manufacturing sector and strong performance in financial and other services. And, like in other advanced societies, government, healthcare and education play an important role in the economy.

GDP

Gross Domestic Product represents the total value of goods and services produced.

- Total Manitoba GDP (2006): $44.85 billion
- GDP per capita: $35,634
- Canadian GDP per capita: $42,464
- Real Manitoba GDP growth (2007): 3.1 percent
- Real Canadian GDP growth (2007): 2.6 percent

Source: Statistics Canada.

TAXES

- Provincial sales tax: 7 percent
- GST (federal sales tax): 5 percent
- Personal income tax rate: 10.9 percent on the first $30,544 of taxable income; 12.75 percent on the amount between $30,545 and $65,000, and 17.4 percent on the amount over $65,000.
- Small business tax rate: 2 percent
- Corporate tax rate: 13 percent

Source: Government of Manitoba.

You Said How Much?

All figures are hourly and are drawn from the latest available data.

Dentists	$59.62
Lawyers	$40.05
University professors	$37.98
School principals & administrators, elementary & secondary education	$36.06
Air pilots, flight engineers & flight instructors	$32.68
Software engineers	$31.73
Economists	$31.25
Registered nurses	$30.63
Pharmacists	$29.62
Police officers (non commissioned)	$28.85
Civil engineers	$28.65
Occupational therapists	$27.00
Fire fighters	$26.92
Aircraft mechanics & inspectors	$25.48
Architects	$25.00
Correctional service officers	$23.08
Librarians	$22.50
Grain elevator operators	$22.02
Social workers	$22.02
Translators, terminologists & interpreters	$21.63
Loan officers	$20.43
Ministers of religion	$20.24
Web designers & developers	$19.71
Truck drivers	$18.22
Graphic designers	$18.03
Chefs	$17.55
Paralegals	$17.31
Auto & truck mechanics	$16.83
Writers	$16.83
Bricklayers	$16.01
Medical secretaries	$15.24
Dancers	$14.90
Restaurant and food service managers	$14.42
Security guards & related occupations	$13.30
Bakers	$12.21
General farm workers	$12.00
Pet groomers & animal care workers	$10.94

Source: Human Resources and Development Canada.

TAX FREEDOM DAY (2007)

Tax freedom day is the date on which earnings no longer go to taxes. June 20 is the date for Canada as a whole.

- Alberta: June 1
- New Brunswick: June 14
- Prince Edward Island: June 14
- Saskatchewan: June 14

 **Bio PETER NYGÅRD**

It's appropriate that Peter Nygård represents a rags to riches story -- he is, after all, a clothing magnate. Born in Finland, as a boy Nygård moved to tiny Deloraine, MB, where his family initially lived without electricity or running water. Today, Nygård lives on his own Bahamian Island (Nygård Cay) in a 150,000 square foot abode second in size only to Buckingham Palace for a private residence.

Modest and self-effacing are not words typically used to describe Nygård, whose Mayan inspired complex was featured on "Lifestyles of the Rich and Famous" and has a 30-car garage, 22 bedrooms, and an interior lagoon. Nygård has played host to heads of state including George Bush Sr., as well as stars like Oprah and Robert De Niro.

But Nygård isn't in the Bahamas just to play and hob nob — he puts in long days in a tree house office that is reached by cable car. Nygård also likes to flaunt the bling in his home town, tooling about in a Rolls during the six weeks per year he spends in Winnipeg, and displaying his oversized photo about the city, notably at his 12,000 square foot flagship store in the West Broadway neighborhood, and at the Nygård Fashion Store in Kenaston Commons.

Nygård's personal life has made for juicy tabloid fodder. Father of seven children by four different women, in 2003 Nygård was involved

- **Manitoba: June 16**
- British Columbia: June 16
- Ontario: June 19
- Nova Scotia: June 19
- Quebec: June 26
- Newfoundland and Labrador: July 1

Source: The Fraser Institute.

in a four-year child support battle with a former Air Canada flight attendant who is the mother of his son. The woman accused Nygård of neglecting the teenaged boy and chiseling on his maintenance, while Nygård tabbed her a gold digger and expressed concern that too much money would spoil the lad. The matter was eventually settled out of court, and the ordeal caused Nygård to lobby the government for changes to Canadian divorce laws.

Nygård's women's fashion empire began in 1967 when he used his life savings and an $8,000 loan to buy 20 percent of a clothing company. He soon owned the firm outright, and Nygård International now has yearly North American sales of one billion dollars. The company is known for its use of high technology in clothing design, manufacture and sales.

Nygård is Canada's top sportswear manufacturer and ranks third in North America. The company has a major presence in Winnipeg, where it employs 1,500, and also has corporate offices in Toronto and New York's Times Square. And boss Nygård apparently has a soft side, the company's well publicized "Nygård for Life" program donates millions annually to fund breast cancer research and awareness.

HOUSEHOLD INCOME AFTER TAXES

The real median household income in Canada after taxes was $45,900 in 2005.

Newfoundland	$37,200
Prince Edward Island	$40,700
Nova Scotia	$39,800
New Brunswick	$38,300

Bio IZZY ASPER

Israel "Izzy" Asper was born in Minnedosa, MB, in 1932, the son of musicians who owned the local theatre, and later two Winnipeg cinemas. At the time of Asper's 2003 death, he was worth over $600 million and was head of an international media and communications empire. The outspoken Asper wore many hats throughout his life: lawyer, politician, newspaper columnist and finally, media mogul. Politically, Asper was a Liberal, and headed the Manitoba Liberal Party from 1970-75, sitting as an MLA from 1972-1975.

A chain smoker, heavy drinker and lover of 1920s era jazz, Asper made his mark when he established a bare bones Winnipeg television station in the 1970s, using equipment he bought from a failing North Dakota operation. Soon after, he purchased the Toronto-based Global Television network, turning the floundering enterprise into a highly profitable chain which turned out original programming and owned many independent stations in western Canada. A 1988 court win for Asper over fellow investors for control of Global paved the way for the CanWest Global juggernaut of the 1990s. The company owns Global Television and E!, as well as a number of prominent

Quebec	$39,200
Ontario	$51,500
Manitoba	**$42,500**
Saskatchewan	$41,300
Alberta	$55,200
British Columbia	$46,500

Source: Canada Mortgage and Housing Corporation.

Canadian newspapers including the *National Post*, the *Montreal Gazette*, the *Ottawa Citizen*, and the *Vancouver Sun*.

CanWest Global also owns the influential US magazine the *New Republic*, and has media and broadcast holdings in countries including the UK, Australia, New Zealand, and Turkey. Izzy's son, Leonard J. Asper, is President and CEO of Winnipeg headquartered CanWest Global, a company which employs nearly 11,000 and posts consolidated annual revenues of nearly three billion dollars.

Asper could be ruthless and overbearing, but he was not afraid to think big, and was a champion of his home province. A fierce critic of the Toronto/Montreal/Ottawa focus of the Canadian media, corporate and political worlds, Asper sought to shift power west.

A graduate of the University of Manitoba, Asper endowed the University's I.H. Asper School of Business to the tune of ten million dollars. The Asper family continues to be a major philanthropic force through the Asper Foundation and the CanWest Global Foundation, which spearheaded the establishment of the Canadian Museum for Human Rights, to be located at the Forks in Winnipeg.

FIVE LARGEST
PRIVATE EMPLOYERS
*Excludes government, crown corporations,
utilities, hospitals and educational institutions.*

1. **Great-West Lifeco** 3,000 (Insurance & Financial Services)
2. **MTS Allstream** 3,000 (Telecommunications)
3. **Kitchen Craft of Canada** 2,100 (Cabinet manufacture)
4. **Palliser Furniture** 1,813 (Furniture manufacture)
5. **The North West Company** 1,474 (Retail)

Source: Manitoba Business Magazine.

LOW INCOME

Eight and a half percent of Manitoban economic families of two persons or more are considered low income, the highest percentage in Canada. The low income rate is a statistical measure indicating a disproportionately large share of income devoted to the necessities of food, shelter and clothing. British Columbia is close behind Manitoba at 8.4 percent, while the neighboring provinces of Saskatchewan and Ontario record low income figures of 7.6 percent and 7.7 percent respectively. The lowest low income rate in Canada is Prince Edward Island at 3.1 percent.

Source: Statistics Canada.

Did you know...

that in 2008 the average car insurance premium in Manitoba was $833? This is the same amount Manitoba Public Insurance charged in 2007, and is among the lowest in Canada.

Take 5 **MARK NEUENDORFF'S TOP FIVE**

**INTERESTING FACTS ABOUT THE ROYAL
CANADIAN MINT'S WINNIPEG FACILITY**

Mark Neuendorff is the Director of the Royal Canadian Mint's
Winnipeg facility. The Mint is a Crown Corporation and was established in Ottawa in 1908. The Winnipeg operation officially opened
in 1976, and now produces all of Canada's circulation coins.

1. **High-speed production** – The Royal Canadian Mint's state-of-the-
art facility in Winnipeg operates 24 hours a day and houses over 40
high-speed coining presses which each strike up to 850 coins a
minute. On an average day they are producing 20 million coins!

2. **International player** – The Royal Canadian Mint's Winnipeg facility not only makes all of Canada's circulation coins, it has also mint-
ed coins for over 70 countries around the world. In 2008, Winnipeg
produced coins for countries including Oman, the United Arab
Emirates, Barbados, Ghana, the Bahamas, Paraguay, the Dominican
Republic and New Zealand.

3. **Golden opportunity** – Canada's oldest and largest gold refinery
has operated at the Royal Canadian Mint's Ottawa headquarters
since 1911. To promote this important part of the Mint's business,
visitors to the Winnipeg facility are welcome to hold in their very
own hands (next to armed security personnel of course) an 11.3 kg
(400 oz) pure gold bar worth almost $400,000!

4. **Standing out from the crowd** – Designed by world renowned
local architect Étienne Gaboury, the Winnipeg Mint's building is a
genuine landmark. The 34 metre tall glass tower, located on 61
hectares of grassland and lakes, peers over the prairie landscape
and is a beacon of Canadian innovation and technology.

5. **It's something to remember** – In 2004, the Winnipeg Mint created the first ever coloured circulation coin. The 25 cent piece was
created in connection with Remembrance Day; it honours Canada's
veterans with a red poppy embedded in a Maple Leaf and the
inscription "Remember/Souvenir."

The Richardson Family

The Richardson empire began in Kingston, Ontario in 1857 when Irish-born James Richardson, a tailor turned grain merchant, founded the company that still bears his name. An orphan who was raised by his aunt, Richardson's ties to the prairies began when his company started selling western Canadian wheat to Europe in the 1880s. The Richardsons built their first Manitoba grain elevator in 1890 in Neepawa, and would go on to construct numerous grain warehouses and elevators in western Canada.

The Richardsons are still major players in the grain business; however, agricultural commodities are just one aspect of the family fortune. The Richardsons diversified early on, entering into the transportation, oil and gas, real estate and finance arenas. In the 1920s, they established Western Canada Airways and Canadian Airways, as well as inaugurating a Moose Jaw radio station, the flagship of a prairie-based network it eventually sold.

Financing operations propelled the company from regional and national player to global presence. Initially, the firm lent money to farm clients, but soon it was competing with the major players in the field. In 1982, the Richardsons merged their finance operations with Greenshields Company Inc., creating financial titan Richardson Greenshields, which was sold in 1996.

James Richardson & Sons remains privately owned, and its president and CEO is Hartley T. Richardson, the seventh Richardson in 150 years to assume that position. The firm has long had an interest in philanthropy, and its charitable foundation was inaugurated in 1957 in commemoration of the 100th anniversary of the company's founding.

You won't go far in Winnipeg without stumbling across the Richardson name, starting with the city's airport, James Armstrong Richardson International. Another landmark is the company's downtown headquarters, the 34-storey Richardson Building at Portage and Main, part of the 4.5 acre Richardson-owned Lombard Place commercial complex.

Take 5

TOP FIVE DESTINATIONS
OF MANITOBA EXPORTS

1. **United States** $8,596 million
2. **Japan** $469 million
3. **China** $349 million
4. **Mexico** $209 million
5. **Hong Kong** $204 million

Source: Government of Manitoba Competitiveness, Training and Trade.

EMPLOYMENT (2008)

Over 600,000 Manitobans are employed; here's how it breaks down (figures are in thousands).

Men	323.8
Women	277.6
Full-Time	489.1
Part-Time	112.3
Self	87.3

Did you know...

that the value of metals and minerals mined in Manitoba in 2006 was $2.6 billion? Nickel, petroleum, zinc and copper lead the way, but there are also Manitoba gold mines. The towns of Flin Flon, Thompson, and Snow Lake in the north, and Bissett in the south are the major mining communities. When activities related to mineral extraction, smelting and processing are combined, they amount to between 4 percent and 5 percent of provincial GDP.

Take 5 TOP FIVE IMPORTS

1. **Bulldozers**	$448 million
2. **Tractors**	$392 million
3. **Cars**	$382 million
4. **Trucks**	$279 million
5. **Harvest equipment**	$278 million
5. **Vehicle parts**	$278 million

Source: Government of Manitoba Competitiveness, Training and Trade.

JOB GROWTH

Manitoba added 1,700 new jobs in 2007, an increase of 1.7 percent over the previous year, the same rate for Canada as a whole in 2007.

UNEMPLOYMENT (FEBRUARY 2008)

- Unemployed: 26,400
- Unemployment rate: 4.2 percent
- Canada's unemployment rate: 5.8 percent

Did you know...

that K-Tel International, famous for hawking music compilations in the "all the number one hits by the number one stars" vein is a family-owned Manitoba business? The operation is run by Winnipeg's Kives family, and K-Tel is short for "Kives Television." In the 1970s, in addition to hawking LPs, 8-tracks and cassettes, K-Tel also sold kitchen and home gadgets, and in the 1980s got into real estate, software, movies and other endeavors. The company went under in 1985, but was reborn in the 1990s. The 1970s voice of K-Tel was Bob Washington, an announcer at Winnipeg radio station CKRC.

Take 5 TOP FIVE EXPORT COMMODITIES

1. **Nickel**	$918 million
2. **Electrical energy**	$648 million
3. **Wheat**	$592 million
4. **Pharmaceuticals for retail sale**	$555 million
5. **Copper**	$423 million

Source: Government of Manitoba Competitiveness, Training and Trade.

BY THE HOUR AND BY THE WEEK

Average weekly earnings in December 2007 were $721.35, and as of February 2008, workers in Manitoba had an average hourly wage of $19.31, up from $18.20 in February 2007, a 6.1 percent increase. The average Canadian hourly wage was $21.14 (February 2008), up from $20.15 in February 2007, a 4.9 percent increase.

- Aged 15 to 24: $11.27
- Aged 25 to 54: $20.94
- Aged 55 and older: $21.65
- Part-time: $14.52
- Full-time: $20.49
- Unionized: $22.17
- Non-unionized: $17.53
- Minimum wage: $8.50

Source: Statistics Canada.

Did you know...

that the Winnipeg suburb of Tuxedo placed tenth on AskMen.com's 2008 ranking of Canada's richest neighborhoods?

Michael Benarroch, Ph.D., is Dean of the Faculty of Business and Economics at the University of Winnipeg. Dr. Benarroch grew up in Winnipeg and received his Ph.D. from Ottawa's Carleton University. He has written widely on the Manitoba economy and other topics for scholarly and government publications, and is frequently interviewed on radio and television. Dr. Benarroch served on the *Encyclopedia of Manitoba's* editorial board, as well as writing its "Economy of Manitoba" entry.

1. **Diversification**. One of the great strengths of the Manitoba economy is its lack of reliance on any one sector. The fastest growing sector, manufacturing, generates 13 percent of the province's GDP, and is led, although not dominated by, food and beverage processing which comprises one quarter of Manitoba's manufactured goods. While Manitoba's diversified economy has allowed it to avoid major economic downturns, the challenge for the province is the absence of a single sector that can drive growth to the levels experienced elsewhere in Canada. As a result, Manitoba's per capita income has remained below the national average.

2. **The Changing Nature of Economy**. Throughout most of the 1900s, natural resources, agriculture (wheat), electricity and primary metals dominated the provincial economic landscape. Also, in the early 1900s Manitoba became the railway transportation hub of Canada. Between 1984 and 2000, however, agriculture and mining, together with fishing, hunting, logging and forestry, declined in prominence, and wheat fell behind oilseeds and hogs among agricultural products. Additionally, finance, insurance and real estate grew in importance, and the low value of the Canadian dollar in the 1990s helped the manufacturing sector more than double in size, changing the landscape from a resource based to a service and manufacturing based economy. The challenge for Manitoba will be its ability to maintain high levels of growth in manufacturing in the face of a rising Canadian dollar.

3. **International Trade**. Exports have been an important engine of growth for the Manitoba economy. Between 1995 and 2007, the value of Manitoba's international exports more than doubled in value. Compared to the rest of Canada, however, exports as a percentage of GDP are considerably lower in Manitoba (26 percent) than for the country as a whole (40 percent). Given the strong Canadian dollar, the main challenge for Manitoba is taking advantage of world export markets to the same extent as the rest of Canada.

4. **Transfer Payments**. Manitoba is a recipient of federal transfer payments that equalize the fiscal capacity of the province with those of richer Canadian provinces. In 2007, Manitoba received $1.54 billion in transfers, the second largest payment in Canada. A major issue for Manitoba has been its inability to keep pace with economic growth in the rest of Canada; consequently it has become reliant on transfer payments to sustain its economy. The challenge facing the province is generating sufficient wealth to eventually become independent of transfer payments.

5. **Hydroelectricity**. Manitoba is a major hydroelectric producer, and plans to double its hydroelectric capacity by 2025. Sixty-six percent of all electricity generated in Manitoba is consumed within the province, with the remainder being exported. While Manitoba charges market rates for its exports, Manitobans pay a rate below market value. The effect of this pricing policy has led Manitobans to be among the highest consumers of electricity in the world, and reduced the amount of electricity available for export. Unlike other provinces that have been able to fully take advantage of rising market prices for their natural resources, Manitoba has undervalued one of its most valuable resources, thereby limiting its ability to fully capitalize on the resource's potential.

They Said It

GENDER GAP

- Percentage of working age men who have jobs: 72.1
- Percentage of working age women who have jobs: 60.9
- Men's average hourly wage: $20.70
- Women's average hourly wage: $17.87
- Women's earnings as a percentage of men's: 86

Source: Statistics Canada.

Did you know...

that in 2006 Manitoba recorded an average of 8.1 days lost per worker due to illness or disability? The Canadian average was 7.6; Alberta and Ontario recorded the lowest figures at 6.6 days annually, while New Brunswick topped the nation at calling in sick with 9.7 days lost.

Did you know...

that Montreal liquor barons the Bronfmans got their start in Manitoba? The Bronfmans opened a hotel in Emerson in 1903, making much of their money from alcohol sales. Sam Bronfman (1889-1971), the architect of the Seagram empire, would go on to become a Winnipeg hotelier, and met his wife, Plum Coulee-born Saidye Rosner, in the city. The family lived in Winnipeg's North End, and did not move to Montreal until the 1920s.

TOP FIVE PLANT CROPS
(2007 FARM RECEIPTS)

1. **Canola**	$308 million
2. **Wheat**	$200 million
3. **Potatoes**	$79 million
4. **Barley**	$31 million
5. **Dry Beans**	$31 million

THE UPPER ECHELON

Four Manitoba families figured in *Canadian Business's* 2005 "The Rich 100" listing:

- **# 22 The Richardson Family**, Winnipeg (agri-business, real estate, petroleum and related businesses). Net worth: $2 billion.
- **# 64 The Asper Family**, Winnipeg (media). Net worth: $833 million.
- **# 80 Peter Nygard**, Bahamas; Winnipeg (clothing, fashion). Net worth: $662 million.
- **# 82 Randall Moffat**, Winnipeg (communications, media). Net worth: $661 million.

HOW WINNIPEGGERS GET TO WORK

- 70 percent drive
- 8.4 percent are automobile passengers
- 13.2 percent use public transit
- 6.1 percent walk
- 1.4 percent bicycle

Source: Statistics Canada.

Take 5

MAKIN' STUFF - TOP FIVE
MANUFACTURING SECTORS

Manufacturing constitutes 13 percent of Manitoba's GDP, and employs about 72,000 people. Major areas of manufactured goods include:

1. **Food Processing.** Food and beverage processing accounts for 25 percent of Manitoba manufacturing shipments, and represents 10,500 jobs. Major items include meat, poultry, dairy products, and flour and feed. Pork, egg and potato processing are particular areas of strength, and major companies include Maple Leaf, McCain, and Archer Daniels Midland. The University of Manitoba and several research institutes engage in food processing R & D.

2. **Transportation Equipment.** Monster machines account for shipments of approximately $2.4 billion annually and 9,000 jobs. The manufacture of buses is the major component, but other products include fire engines, motor homes and semi-trailers. Manitoba companies produce over one third of North American buses, with New Flyer and Motor Coach Industries leading the way.

3. **Building and Finished Wood Products.** This sector is responsible for sales of more than $1.4 billion annually and 13,000 jobs. Major items include furniture, cabinetry, windows, doors, building components and other converted wood products. Chief firms include Canada's largest furniture manufacturer, Palliser Furniture, and Canada's largest kitchen cabinet manufacturer, Kitchen Craft Cabinetry.

4. **Aerospace.** Four firms – Boeing, Standard Aero, Magellan/Bristol Aerospace and Air Canada Technical Services dominate the field, and the sector generates revenues of more than $1.3 billion yearly and 5,000 jobs.

5. **Agribusiness & Manufacturing Technology.** This area includes the manufacture of equipment, machinery and parts for agricultural production, transportation and storage, and accounts for 6,000 jobs. About 70 percent of such goods are exported, principally to the US.
Source: Government of Manitoba Competitiveness, Training and Trade.

They Said It

WHERE THE MONEY GOES

Manitoba households spent an average of $59,230 a year in 2006. Here's how it broke down:

- Income tax: $12,282 (20.7 percent of total spending)
- Shelter: $10,176 (17.2 percent)
- Transportation: $8,113 (13.7 percent)
- Food: $6,101(10.3 percent)
- Insurance/pension payments: $3,700 (6.2 percent)
- Recreation: $3,287 (5.5 percent)
- Household operation: $2,782 (4.7 percent)
- Clothing: $2,346 (4.0 percent)
- Monetary gifts/contributions: $2,248 (3.8 percent)
- Health care: $1,728 (2.9 percent)
- Tobacco and alcohol: $1,382 (2.3 percent)
- Personal care: $1,017 (1.7 percent)
- Education: $909 (1.5 percent)
- Games of chance: $300 (0.5 percent)
- Reading material: $ 257 (0.4 percent)

Source: Statistics Canada.

Did you know...

that the median amount given to charity by a Manitoban taxfiler was $310 in 2006, the same figure as for Ontario and Saskatchewan? The median for Canada as a whole was $250; Quebecers were the stingiest with a median amount donated of $130, while residents of Nunavut were the most generous, giving $450.

HOME SWEET HOME

Affordable housing is one of Manitoba's hallmarks. At the end of 2007, the average Manitoba home price was $169,189, ($174,500 in the city of Winnipeg). British Columbia topped the nation with average digs costing $439,123, while Newfoundland was the cheapest at $149,258. Saskatchewan was comparable to Manitoba with an average home price of $174,405.

Source: Canada Mortgage and Housing Corporation.

Putting Bread on the Table:
The Canadian Wheat Board

The Canadian Wheat Board (CWB) was formed in 1935, and functions as a marketing agency for wheat and barley growers in western Canada. Its origins date to the 1905 Grain Growers' Grain Company.

The Winnipeg headquartered CWB has a monopoly on the sale of western Canada grain, and employs about 500 people in Winnipeg, Vancouver, Tokyo and Beijing. 2006 CWB revenues totaled $4.95 billion, with $4.53 billion of that amount distributed back to farmers.

The Board's monopoly power has occasionally proved unpopular — some western Canadian farmers are opposed to it, as is the US which believes it constitutes a trade barrier. The World Trade Organization ruled against the US on this matter in 2003. Canada's Conservative government is also not a fan of the CWB in its current form, and has sought to overhaul it. The current CWB head honcho is Ian White, an import from Down Under who previously served as head of Queensland Sugar in Brisbane, Australia.

Did you know...

that Winnipeg communications titan Randall Moffat's $100 million gift to the Winnipeg Foundation in 2001 represented the second largest charitable donation in Canadian history?

RENTING

The average monthly rent in Winnipeg in 2007 was $740, and the vacancy rate was 1.5 percent. Rents in selected other Canadian cities (2007):

Vancouver	$1,084
Edmonton	$958
Regina	$656
Toronto	$1,061
Montreal	$647
Halifax	$815
St. John's	$614

Source: Statistics Canada.

Did you know...

that hogs are Manitoba's top livestock crop, and Brandon is a leading hog-butchering centre? Maple Leaf Foods is Brandon's largest employer, and by the end of 2009 it will process 89,000 hogs per week at its Brandon plant. Maple Leaf has recruited workers from countries including Columbia, Mexico, Ukraine and China to fill its manpower needs.

They Said It

WHAT DO YOU DO ALL DAY? MANITOBANS ON THE JOB

In February 2008, 601,400 Manitobans were employed — here's what they were doing. Figures are in thousands.

- **Retail and wholesale sales and trade:** 86.8 (14.4 percent of total employment)
- **Healthcare and social assistance:** 75.3 (12.5 percent)
- **Manufacturing:** 71.8 (11.9 percent)
- **Education:** 44.5 (7.4 percent)
- **Accommodation and food services:** 38.4 (6.4 percent)
- **Finance, insurance, real estate:** 38.1 (6.3 percent)
- **Public administration:** 37.3 (6.2 percent)
- **Transportation and warehousing:** 35.9 (6.0 percent)
- **Construction:** 35.3 (5.9 percent)
- **Professional, scientific & technical services:** 28.2 (4.7 percent)
- **Other services:** 26.7 (4.4 percent)
- **Information, culture, recreation:** 25.7 (4.3 percent)
- **Business, building and other support services:** 18.7 (3.1 percent)
- **Forestry, fishing, mining, oil & gas:** 6.1 (1.0 percent)
- **Utilities:** 5.5 (0.9 percent)

Source: Statistics Canada.

BUSINESSES: SMALL, MEDIUM & LARGE

Manitoba had 36,404 businesses in 2007, over half of which comprised four employees or less. Small businesses (less than 100 employees) constituted 97.3 of total Manitoba businesses, and represented 20 percent of Manitoba GDP (2005). Medium sized operations (100-499 employees) were 2.4 percent of the total, and large businesses (500+ employees) amounted to only .3 percent of total businesses. Large enterprises are major employers; however, accounting for about half of total jobs.

Source: Statistics Canada.

THEY TREAT YOU RIGHT

Seven Manitoba firms made *Maclean's* Top 100 Employers list. These were the companies that provided workers innovative perks like pet insurance, low interest home loans, and birthdays off, as well as more traditional benefits in the areas of retirement, education and parental leave.

- **Boeing Canada** (Aircraft manufacture)
- **New Flyer Industries** (Bus manufacture)
- **Ceridian Canada** (Human resources management)
- **Wardrop Engineering**
- **Manitoba Liquor Control Commission**
- **Assiniboine Credit Union**
- **Monsanto Canada** (Agricultural research)

Source: Maclean's.

Did you know...

that in 2007, the federal government employed 11,800 people in Winnipeg? This figure represents three percent of total employment in the city, and is the tenth highest percentage among 33 Canadian census metropolitan areas (CMAs). Not surprisingly, Ottawa had the highest percentage of federal employees among Canadian CMAs at 18 percent.

LET IT RIDE

The Manitoba Lotteries Corporation (MLC) had total revenues of nearly $700 million in 2006-07, and a net income of $282.7 million. The MLC distributes and sells lottery tickets, and owns and operates two Winnipeg casinos as well as a province-wide video lottery terminal network. Manitoba households reported spending $300 (net) on games of chance in 2006.

THE JUICE BUSINESS

Manitoba Hydro, a provincial Crown Corporation, is one of Canada's largest utilities and a major exporter of electricity.

Employees	6,000
2007 total revenues	$2.14 billion
2007 net income	$122 million
Capital assets	$11 billion
Electricity generated annually	30 billion kilowatt hours
2006-07 export sales	$827 million (80 percent to the US market; 20 percent to Canada)

Sources: Manitoba Hydro; Manitoba Business Magazine.

PUBLIC ADMINISTRATION AND BEYOND

In 2007, 152,014 Manitobans worked in the public sector, which includes not only government workers, but also government business enterprises like Canada Post and the Royal Canadian Mint, and those employed in the areas of education and healthcare.

Source: Statistics Canada.

PLANES, TRAINS, TRUCKS AND SHIPS

Manitoba sits in the middle of the North American continent and has long been a transportation hub.

Road: The trucking industry employs 33,000 Manitobans, and hauls 95 percent of land freight. Ninety percent of Manitoba trucking firms operate inter-provincially or internationally.

Rail: CN and Canadian Pacific have a combined 3,900 km of track, and a number of regional railways operate another 1,800 km of track. CN and CP both operate intermodal terminals in which containers and trailers are transferred between road and rail.

Water: The Port of Churchill on Hudson Bay has four deep sea berths and is connected by rail to the southern part of the province. It is chiefly used to ship grain.

Air: Winnipeg's James Armstrong Richardson International Airport generates approximately 20,000 jobs and ships over 140,000 metric tonnes of cargo annually. Passenger traffic in 2007 was 3.57 million, an increase of 5.6 percent from 2006.

Weblinks

Manitoba Competitiveness, Training and Trade
www.gov.mb.ca/ctt/index.html
A Government of Manitoba site with a wealth of information and statistics on the Manitoba economy, including trade, investment, employment, industry, and small and large businesses.

Winnipeg Chamber of Commerce
www.winnipeg-chamber.com
The voice of Winnipeg's business community, the "About Winnipeg" section of the "About Us" section has excellent information on the city and its economy.

Politics

Whether it's because of the multicultural nature of a province that served as gateway for western immigration in the late 1800s, or the historic tension between First Nations, English Protestants and Francophone Catholics, Manitoba politics have always had a defiant, progressive nature. Manitoba spawned women's suffrage in Canada, sowed the seeds of an agrarian movement and was the scene of a famous general strike.

VIOLENCE ROCKS THE RED RIVER COLONY

Conflict and strife defined Manitoba's early history. Even before the Scottish settlers and the Métis clashed during the Red River Rebellion, political life in the Red River Valley was anything but tranquil.

Officers of the Hudson's Bay Company (HBC) were the first Europeans to impose political control over an area that was previously the domain of Cree and Ojibway First Nations. The company established a system of forts, governors and agents to manage trade in what was then known as Rupert's Land. Competitors from the North West Company ran a number of rival posts, mostly in the southern area near the US border.

In 1811, the HBC granted 300,000 km of land in the Lake Winnipeg Basin to Thomas Douglas, the fifth Earl of Selkirk. Dubbing the region "Assiniboia," Lord Selkirk promptly arranged for a group of Scottish settlers to establish a base near the junction of the Red and Assiniboine rivers, the site of contemporary Winnipeg.

The settlers were unable to sustain themselves through the harsh winter, and turned for help to French Canadian North West Company traders living in the region. Relations were good until the Selkirk-appointed governor, Miles MacDonell, issued the Pemmican Proclamation in 1814. The law, which was an effort to ensure settlers a steady supply of food, forbade the export of provisions from the region, thus preventing North West traders from supplying their canoe brigades.

Alarmed that the Scottish settlers were trying to control their land, the Nor'Westers and their Métis allies retaliated, burning the settlement. The rivalry between the North West Company and HBC escalated, and forts were seized and burned by both companies.

Selkirk brought in more settlers and a new governor, Robert Semple, further straining relations and culminating in the 1816 Massacre at Seven Oaks. Led by Cuthbert Grant, the Métis killed Semple and 19 men the HBC had sent to protect the settlers.

Attacks and counterattacks followed, along with lawsuits and counterlawsuits, all of which finally came to an end with the death of Selkirk in 1820 and the merger of the rival trading companies in 1821. In 1836, the HBC took possession of the struggling colony, but was not always successful in maintaining control of commerce and trade.

By the late 1860s, Manitoba was being wooed by the expansionist ambitions of the Americans to the south. In response, the HBC agreed to sell its remaining lands to the government in Ottawa, thus putting in motion a series of events that would lead to Manitoba's violent birth.

Did you know...

that Manitoba was known as the "postage stamp province" because it was originally square and covered only the southern 40 percent of the province's present territory? The borders were extended to the current size in 1912.

They Said It

"We are not here to play politics or to represent a single class, but to get down to the serious business of giving this province an efficient government."

– Premier John Bracken, voicing his non-partisan philosophy to the Manitoba Legislature in 1923.

GOVERNMENT DOUGH:
WHERE MANITOBA GETS ITS CASH (2007-08)

- Total revenue: $11.8 billion
- Percentage from income taxes: 20.7 percent
- Other taxes: 27.5 percent
- Fees and other revenue: 10.3 percent
- Net income of government business and enterprises: 5.8 percent
- Sinking funds and other earnings: 4.5 percent
- Federal transfers: 31.2 percent

SPENDING THE DOUGH:
WHERE MANITOBA SPENDS ITS CASH (2007-08)

- Total expenditures: $11.6 billion
- Health: 35.1 percent
- Education: 26.7 percent
- Family services and housing: 10.8 percent
- Debt charges: 7.4 percent
- Community, Economic and Resource Development: 11.9 percent
- Justice and other expenditures: 8.1 percent

DEBT

Total provincial debt (2006-07): 11.13 billion
Percent of GDP: 24.2
Debt per person: $9,325
Surplus for 2007-08: $175 million

Source: Government of Manitoba.

MANITOBA PREMIERS AND THEIR OCCUPATIONS

Premier	Party	Term	Occupation
Alfred Boyd	n/a	1870-1871	merchant
Marc-Amable Girard	n/a	1871-1872	lawyer
Marc-Amable Girard	n/a	1874	lawyer
Henry Hynes Clarke	n/a	1872-1874	lawyer, journalist
Robert Atkinson Davis	n/a	1874-1878	businessman
John Norquay	Cons	1878-1887	teacher, farmer
David Howard Harrison	Cons	1887-1888	doctor
Thomas Greenway	Lib	1888-1900	merchant, reeve, farmer
Hugh John Macdonald	Cons	1900	lawyer
Rodmond Palen Roblin	Cons	1900-1915	farmer
Tobias Crawford Norris	Lib	1915-1922	farmer, auctioneer
John Bracken	Lib-Prog	1922-1943	professor
Stuart Sinclair Garson	Lib-Prog	1943-1948	lawyer
Douglas Lloyd Campbell	Lib-Prog	1948-1958	farmer, teacher
Dufferin Roblin	PC	1958-1967	businessman
Walter C. Weir	PC	1967-1969	funeral director, alderman
Edward R. Schreyer	NDP	1969-1977	professor
Sterling Rufus Lyon	PC	1977-1981	lawyer, judge
Howard Pawley	NDP	1981-1988	lawyer
Gary Filmon	PC	1988-1999	civil engineer
Gary Doer	NDP	1999-	corrections officer, union leader

Did you know...

that Saskatchewan's pride, Scottish-born Tommy Douglas, was raised in Winnipeg? Douglas earned a bachelor's degree from Brandon College, where he was friends with fellow prairie social democrat Stanley Knowles. Douglas, who was the grandfather of actor Kiefer Sutherland, was a Baptist minister in Carberry, MB after leaving Brandon. He settled in Saskatchewan in 1930.

THE MANITOBA SCHOOLS QUESTION

Manitoba entered confederation with a population precariously balanced between English Protestants and French Catholics. Up to 1878, the seats in the provincial legislature were almost equally divided between English and French, as were cabinet portfolios.

However, when the combined English and immigrant population overtook the number of Francophones, the English no longer saw the need for power sharing. In 1890, the Legislature passed a bill establishing English as Manitoba's official language. All government business was to be conducted in English only, and bills and legislation recorded solely in English as well.

The separate school system, the last bastion of Francophone rights, was the next to fall. The School Act of 1890 dissolved the church-dominated school system, replacing it with a public, non-sectarian English-only system funded by property taxes.

Manitoba's French Catholics challenged the law on the grounds that it

Take 5 J.M. BUMSTED'S FIVE
WATERSHED EVENTS IN MANITOBA'S POLITICAL HISTORY

Dr. John M. (Jack) Bumsted is the author of many popular and scholarly books on Canadian history, including *Floods of the Centuries*, *The Red River Rebellion*, *The Winnipeg General Strike of 1919*, and *Dictionary of Manitoba Biography*. Professor Bumsted recently retired from a long academic career at University of Manitoba. He now devotes his time to his Whodunit Mystery Bookstore and his role as President of the Manitoba Historical Society.

1. **The Red River Uprising of 1869-70**
2. **The Manitoba Schools Crisis of the early 1890s**
3. **The Winnipeg General Strike of 1919**
4. **The Floodway debate of the early 1960s**
5. **The Schreyer NDP victory of 1969**

violated both the British North America Act of 1867 and the Manitoba Act of 1870. The Schools Question and the issue of minority rights was debated for several years in both Manitoba and Ottawa, but the federal

Bio LOUIS RIEL, FATHER OF MANITOBA

One of the most controversial figures in Canadian history, Riel is widely recognized as the founder of Manitoba. The eldest of 11 children in a prominent Métis family, he was born at the Red River Settlement in 1844. At 14, he moved to Montreal to continue the education he started in St. Boniface, returning in 1868 upon the death of his father.

Shortly thereafter, Riel became embroiled in the Métis opposition to Canada's annexation of Rupert's Land from the Hudson's Bay Company. An 1869 land survey fueled Métis fears of losing their traditional lands, and prompted Riel to form the National Committee. Under his leadership, the French Catholic Métis launched the Red River Rebellion, turning back the survey party and assuming control of Upper Fort Garry at the forks of the Red and Assiniboine rivers.

Inviting the participation of both French and English settlers, Riel then formed and led a Provisional Government that presented the Federal Government with a "List of Rights." Based on this list, Ottawa passed the Manitoba Act in May 1870, effectively establishing the new province.

Riel's tenure as president of the provisional government was marred by his decision to sanction the execution of Thomas Scott, an Orangeman and agitator during the Rebellion. Driven into exile due to the incident, Riel relocated to Montana where he married and eventually became a US citizen. In 1875, Ottawa granted Riel amnesty on the condition he remain in exile for five more years.

government failed to compel the province to change the legislation. It was not until 1985 that French language rights were legally restored in the areas of law, justice and education.

During his exile, Riel became increasingly convinced of his destiny as the messiah of the Métis. In June 1884, he accepted a request from settlers in the Saskatchewan Valley to lead them in a protest against the Canadian Government for grievances similar to those existing at Red River 14 years earlier.

Riel and his followers were unhappy with the negotiations with Ottawa, and declared a provisional government in 1885. The federal government intervened quickly to put down what was known as the North West Rebellion, and troops loyal to Riel were routed at the Battle of Batoche. Ottawa's quick response proved key in putting down the Rebellion, but the lack of support among English speaking prairie dwellers also doomed the movement.

Riel was tried for treason and hanged at Regina in November 1885. His remains now lie in the cemetery of the St. Boniface Cathedral in Winnipeg. A re-enactment of his trial was broadcast in 2002 on CBC, reopening the debate among those who see him as the father of Manitoba, and others who believe he was a traitor who incited civil war.

For many years after Riel's death, the matter of his legacy broke down along religious and ethnic lines with people of Francophone, Métis and First Nations backgrounds generally favorable to Riel, and Anglos taking a dimmer view of him. These divisions are no longer as sharp as they once were, and in 2007, the Government of Manitoba proclaimed a statutory Louis Riel Day to be held every third Monday in February.

WOMEN IN POLITICS

1887: Women are granted the right to vote in municipal elections, but not to hold office.

1907: Manitoba revokes women's municipal franchise. Public protest reinstates the vote.

1912: Winnipeg writer and activist Nellie McClung helps organize the Political Equality League.

1914: McClung leads a five-person delegation calling on Manitoba premier Rodmond Roblin to grant women the vote. He refuses.

1914: The Women's Parliament is staged at the Walker Theatre.

1915: The Political Equality League submits a petition to government for female suffrage.

1916: Manitoba becomes the first province in Canada to give women the right to vote and run in provincial elections.

1920: Liberal Edith McTavish Rogers becomes the first female MLA in Manitoba.

1960: Olive Lillian Irvine, a Conservative and a teacher from Lisgar, is the first woman to represent Manitoba in Canada's senate.

1963: Margaret Konantz becomes the first Manitoba woman elected to the House of Commons. She is the daughter of Edith Rogers, the first woman MLA in Manitoba.

1971: Jean Folster of Norway House becomes the first woman Chief in Manitoba.

1981: Pearl McGonigal becomes the first woman Lieutenant Governor in Manitoba.

1984: Sharon Carstairs, a Liberal, becomes the first female leader of a Manitoba political party.

FARMERS UNITE

The dawn of the 20th century saw the rise of an agrarian protest movement in Manitoba. High tariffs and freight rates imposed by the federal government prompted farmers to organize under the Manitoba Grain Grower's Association (MGGA).

MGGA members first ventured into politics by throwing their support behind Nellie McClung's successful bid to gain women the vote in 1916. After World War I, their focus shifted to lobbying both provincial and federal governments to improve rural life and reform the grain-marketing system.

When their efforts failed, members reorganized as the United Farmers of Manitoba (UFM), thereby hoping to gain greater rural support and more direct influence on the political process. But unlike the United Farmers of Alberta, the UFM had no interest in partnering with labour politicians. In fact, the Winnipeg General Strike was generally unpopular with farmers who tended to be more right-wing than their counterparts in the other prairie provinces.

In 1920, a number of farmer candidates ran in Manitoba's provincial election. Twelve were elected, eight as members of the UFM, and four as independents. By the time the next election rolled around, two years later, the agrarian movement was picking up steam. In 1922, with no leader, a meager budget and a bare-bones platform, the UFM won handily. The UFM then asked Professor John Bracken to head the party and become premier. The organization also renamed its political wing the Progressive Party of Manitoba to lend it more credibility among non-farming Manitobans.

Although subsequent elections proved more challenging, Bracken's knack for striking alliances with the other parties made him Manitoba's longest-serving premier. He initiated an alliance with the Liberals in the

1920s, and his 1940 wartime coalition government included members of all parties (Conservative, Social Credit and NDP precursor Cooperative Commonwealth Federation).

The Liberal-Progressive alliance, which featured low taxes, restrained spending, and an antipathy to organized labour, ruled from the early 1920s until 1958 when the Conservatives took power. The party dropped the "Progressive" tag and was reborn in 1961 as the Liberal Party of Manitoba.

Take 5 ED SCHREYER'S FIVE
MANITOBANS HE ADMIRES

Born and raised in Beausejour, Edward Schreyer became an MLA at 22 and then, at 33, Manitoba's first New Democratic Premier, holding that office from 1969 to 1977. He served as Governor General of Canada from 1979 to 1984, and then Canadian High Commissioner to Australia, Papua New Guinea, Solomon Islands and Ambassador to Vanuatu until 1988. Today, he is the Chancellor of Brandon University, and also serves as Chairman of the Canadian Association for the Study of Peak Oil and Gas (ASPO Canada), and as a national representative on behalf of Habitat for Humanity International.

1. **Stanley Knowles and Tommy Douglas** were driven by human compassion for lower income families and individuals, as well as the ill and afflicted. Canada's Medicare, along with other major "social net" programs, was enacted in very large part due to their efforts.
2. **Duff Roblin** – I sat "across the aisle" from Premier Roblin from 1958 to 1965 as a 22-to-28 year old enthusiastic participant "under the Dome and the Golden Boy." Roblin and his administration brought Manitoba very effectively into the modern era of post-WWII with a kaleidoscope of desirable changes in education, hospital finance, roads, social assistance and flood protection.
3. **Larry Desjardins** – MLA from 1959 to 1988, he sat as a Liberal for his first ten years, then three years as an Independent and "liberal

POLITICAL GEOGRAPHY
Municipalities: 198
Cities: 9
Towns: 52
Villages: 20
Location of Legislature: 450 Broadway Avenue, Winnipeg

democrat," before joining the NDP caucus in 1973. In keeping with Larry's sense of ethics, he crossed the floor only after obtaining his constituency association's blessing at a large and vocal public meeting. This was entirely without precedent and, considering the centralized control of party machines today, almost certainly couldn't happen again. He was a stalwart defender of the linguistic and cultural heritage of Manitoba francophones.

4. **Dave Courchene** – Courchene was the first spokesman of the Manitoba Indian Brotherhood (MIB) to bring Aboriginal leadership to province-wide and then national attention. He was plainspoken — even blunt — proud and resolute. Equally realistic and practical-minded, he worked cooperatively and effectively with the Government of Manitoba to bring all-weather landing airstrips and winter roads to remote communities of northern and eastern Manitoba.

5. **Manitoba Hydro CEO's Don Stephens, Len Batemen and David Cass-Beggs** – From 1951 to 1978, they coordinated the construction of all Manitoba's modern era hydro-electric generating plants (except Limestone) for a combined average-year generation of 30 million megawatt hours of clean energy (without the 30 million tons of CO_2 that would have been created by coal-fired plants). Manitobans enjoy the lowest electricity rates in North America (and, except for Iceland and Norway, in the world), the ultimate proof of the competence of their work.

Manitobans Taking a Stand

Manitobans have never been afraid of the "good" fight. Ever since Louis Riel stood up for the Métis, many others have carried the torch for justice and equality.

• In 1912, Nellie McClung, as a member of the Political Equity League, led Premier Rodmond Roblin through the city's sweatshops to witness the appalling conditions in which women toiled. When he failed to see the necessity of giving women the vote, she staged a "women's" parliament at Winnipeg's Walker Theatre to mock the premier and his men. By 1916, Manitoba's women were granted the right to vote in provincial elections.

• In 1976, Georges Forest single handedly reversed 89 years of unilingual English policy in Manitoba. What did he do? He challenged a parking ticket written only in English. Three years later, the Supreme Court of Canada declared 4,000 Manitoba laws invalid until they were translated into French. It turns out the 1890 law proclaiming English as the province's only language contravened the 1870 Manitoba Act, and was therefore unconstitutional. The 1979 ruling prompted subsequent provincial governments to expand French-language services. In 1993, a publicly funded Francophone school system was reinstated across the province.

• With an eagle feather in his hand and a look of quiet resolve, Elijah Harper defeated the Meech Lake Accord in 1990. Harper, who was born in 1949 in Red Sucker Lake, a northern Manitoba reserve, had become the first Treaty Indian to be elected as a provincial politician in 1981. The Meech Lake deal to amend the constitution required ratification by all ten provincial legislatures in order to pass. Harper opposed Meech for not allowing adequate participation by Aboriginal people in Canada's political process, including the drafting of the Accord itself. Harper's story was immortalized in the CTV movie *Elijah* in 2007.

They Said It

> "I am glad the Crown have [sic] proved that I am the leader of the half-breeds in the Northwest. I will perhaps be one day acknowledged as more than a leader of the half-breeds, and if I am, I will have an opportunity of being acknowledged as a leader of good in this great country."
>
> **– Louis Riel, 1885**

POLITICAL PARTIES

Manitoba is home to six registered political parties: the Communist Party, the Freedom Party, the Liberal Party, the New Democratic Party, the Green Party and the Progressive Conservative Party. The Liberals, the PCs and the NDP are the only currently existing parties that have ever formed the government. However, in 1922, the United Farmers Party gained support in rural areas and formed an alliance with the Liberals under the Progressive Party banner. Today, the provincial government is headed by the NDP with the Progressive Conservative party in opposition.

PREMIER PRIMER

- Number of Premiers who have served since 1870: 20
- First Conservative Party Premier: John Norquay (1878)
- First Liberal Party Premier: Thomas Greenway (1888)
- First New Democratic Party Premier: Edward R. Schreyer (1969)
- Youngest Premier: Edward R. Schreyer, aged 33
- Oldest Premier: Douglas Lloyd Campbell, aged 63 (at end of term)
- Longest-serving Premier: John Bracken, 20 years
- Shortest-serving Premier: David Howard Harrison. Harrison held the position for a mere 18 days straddling December 1987 and January 1988
- Number of female Premiers: 0
- Number of Premiers born outside the province: 13
- First Premier born in Manitoba: John Norquay

Did you know...

that Stanley Knowles was Manitoba's longest serving MP? He
represented Winnipeg North Centre for almost 38 years between
1942 and 1984 on behalf of the Co-operative Commonwealth
Federation and its successor, the New Democratic Party.

THE CURRENT PROVINCIAL ADMINISTRATION
- Premier: Gary Doer, the 20th
- Party: New Democratic Party of Manitoba
- Date sworn in: October 5, 1999
- Re-elected: June 3, 2003 and May 22, 2007
- Number of MLAs: 57
- Number of NDP seats: 36
- Number of Conservative seats: 19
- Number of Liberal seats: 2
- Number of women MLAs: 17
- Number of residents per MLA: Approximately 20,000
- Lt. Governor: The Honourable John Harvard, P.C., O.M.

FEDERAL POLITICS
- Number of native-born Manitobans who have been Prime Minister: 0
  (Arthur Meighen represented Portage la Prairie while Conservative PM
  in the 1920s, but he was born in Ontario)
- Members of Parliament: 14
- Number who are Conservative: 8
- Number who are Liberal: 3
- Number who are NDP: 3
- Number who are female: 4
- Senators: 6
- Number of female Senators: 4

Duff's Ditch

Dufferin Roblin was born in Winnipeg in 1917, two years after his grandfather, Rodmond Palen Roblin, concluded his term as premier. When his turn came to run for the province's top political office in 1958, "Duff," as people called him, was elected on the promise to provide flood protection to Winnipeg.

The rising waters of the Red River had devastated the city in 1950, and a subsequent Royal Commission recommended the construction of a ditch to divert any future overflow around the city. Roblin, a Progressive Conservative, championed the idea, despite vehement protest by the Liberal opposition. The Liberals objected to the expropriation of surrounding acreage, mostly farmland. Instead, they proposed dredging the river and raising dikes. Jeers directed against "Duff's ditch" and "Duff's folly" filled the legislature. Undeterred, Roblin pressed ahead, breaking sod at the construction site in 1962, his young son in tow. Ultimately, 100 million cubic yards of earth were moved to build the Floodway, an amount greater than the Suez or Panama Canal excavations. More importantly, the Floodway came in under budget, and was opened on October 11, 1968.

The floodway is 47 km long, and almost as wide as the Red River. This engineering wonder was designed to protect Winnipeg from a flood 50 percent greater than the one that hit in 1950. Eventually, the name "Duff's Ditch" became a fond nickname rather than an insult. Between 1968 and 1999, the floodway saved Winnipeg 20 times. In 1997, Roblin was given the honour of raising the floodgates and sparing the city another devastating deluge.

The 1997 flood caused considerable damage and stretched the floodway to its limit. In 2005, the provincial government undertook a substantial widening of the channel, a project which is expected to be completed in spring 2009. Including flood protection measures for rural Manitoba, the cost of the project is pegged at $665 million, a bargain given that the Floodway has prevented over eight billion dollars in damage thus far.

They Said It

FRANCHISE FACTS

- Year responsible government was implemented: 1870
- Year women earned franchise: 1916
- Year First Nations received federal and provincial vote (without renouncing Indian Act status or giving up treaty rights): 1960
- Voting age: 18
- Residency: must be a Manitoba resident for at least 6 months immediately before Election Day

ELECTION DAY

Provincial elections are usually held every four to five years, but can be held at any time in between.

VOTER TURNOUT IN RECENT PROVINCIAL ELECTIONS

- 1995: 69.2 percent
- 1999: 68.1 percent
- 2003: 54.2 percent
- 2007: 56.8 percent

Source: Elections Manitoba.

Did you know...

that Winnipeg was the first Canadian city to have an openly gay mayor? Glen Murray held the job from 1998 to 2004.

MANITOBA'S OTHER FATHER?

Thomas Spence declared himself the president of "Manitobah" in 1867. The unlikely statesman was really a Scottish handyman who came to the area around Portage la Prairie that same year. He wasted no time informing the British Government of his newly created "Republic" of 400 people. The Imperial office promptly denied his petition. His short-lived career as head of the provisional government is immortalized in the National Film Board vignette, "Spence's Republic" (1978).

Weblinks

Office of the Premier
www.gov.mb.ca/minister/premier
Find out everything you ever wanted to know about the premier, the cabinet, and the latest developments at the top of the political process.

Government
www.gov.mb.ca/government
From the lieutenant governor, to the members of the legislative assembly, everyone is listed here, along with every department and policy.

Latest News
http://www.cbc.ca/manitoba/
CBC has its pulse of the latest developments in Manitoba politics, complete with videos and podcasts.

Then and Now

Manitoba's earliest beginnings were marked by struggles against the elements, fierce economic competition, bitter French-English rivalry and a sharp divide between Métis and European visions for the future of the land. After an economic boom in the early part of the 20th century, Manitoba was beset with labour and political unrest culminating in the 1919 General Strike, and then the crushing effects of the Depression which hit the prairies particularly hard.

Is it any wonder, then, that Manitobans have developed into a tenacious and persevering people? Since WWII, Manitoba has experienced relative peace, with moderate economic and population growth and incremental change in the political and social realms.

MANITOBA POPULATION THEN AND NOW

1871	25,228
1881	62,260
1891	152,506
1901	255,211

1911	461,394
1931	700,139
1971	988,247
1996	1,113,898
2001	1,119,583
2007	1,177,800
2008	1,193,566

Source: Statistics Canada.

RURAL-URBAN DIVIDE

	Percent Pop Urban	Percent Pop Rural
1871	4	96
1901	28	72
1931	45	55
1961	64	36
1991	72	28
2001	72	28

Take 5 FIVE MANITOBA FIRSTS

1. Western Canada's first opera house was built in Virden, Manitoba in 1911.
2. The Winnipeg Falcons become the world's first hockey team to win a gold medal, garnering the top spot at the 1920 Olympic Games.
3. Canada's first A&W drive-in opened on Winnipeg's Portage Avenue in 1956.
4. The first Internet pharmacy was launched in Manitoba in 2000.
5. The University of Manitoba became the first university in Canada to offer a doctorate program in peace and conflict studies. Established in 2005, it is one of only 14 such programs offered in the world.

POPULATION DENSITY

	MB p/km²	CAD p/km²
1871	0.04	0.41
1911	0.81	0.80
1931	1.23	1.15
1956	1.55	1.75
1976	1.86	2.49
2006	2.1	3.5

TOP TEN ETHNIC ORIGINS THEN AND NOW

1921	1996	2006
English	English	Canadian
Scottish	Canadian	English
Other Europeans*	German	German
Irish	Scottish	Scottish
French	Ukrainian	Ukrainian
Scandinavian	French	Irish
Dutch	Irish	French
German	Aboriginal	Aboriginal
Jewish	Polish	Polish
Polish	Dutch	Métis

*Other Europeans included Ukrainians, Lithuanians, Russians, and Hungarians.

Source: Statistics Canada.

Did you know...

that Fort Prince of Wales near Churchill was captured by the French in 1783 without a single shot being fired? At the time, the British fort was staffed by only 22 people, most of them tradesmen and labourers.

MINIMUM WAGE

1965	$0.75
1975	$2.75
1985	$4.30
1995	$5.25
2005	$7.25
2008	$8.50

THE CHURCH

Religion played a pivotal role in the lives of early immigrants to Manitoba. For many years, Manitobans were divided along religious lines into Protestants and Catholics; the former typically English-speakers, and the latter, Francophones.

In 1818, Lord Selkirk invited Father Provencher from Montreal to build a Catholic church for the Métis and First Nations people who lived in the area. Not long after, the first Anglican missionary, John West, also came to Red River and built St. John's Church, the first Anglican parish west of the Great Lakes. Despite their differences, from then on Manitoba's Catholics and Anglicans shared a history of church fires and subsequent rebuilding, first in wood and then in stone.

One of the outstanding examples of local church architecture was the striking French Romanesque St. Boniface Cathedral which was completed in 1908. This landmark house of worship burned down in 1968, but a new Cathedral that incorporated some of the old building's façade and walls in its design was erected on the site. Winnipeg's Main Street is the site of another architectural jewel, the onion-domed Holy

Did you know...

that in the 1870s steamboats plied the Red River between Manitoba and the US? Rail transportation soon superseded water traffic, however, and by the 1880s steamboats were in serious decline.

Trinity Metropolitan Cathedral. Built in 1962, it is the seat of the Ukrainian Orthodox Church of Canada.

Despite the drop in church attendance over the years, these icons endure, a testament to the role religion has played in shaping the province.

Take 5 BILL NORRIE'S FIVE THINGS
THAT WERE BETTER IN MANITOBA 50 YEARS AGO

Bill Norrie served as Mayor of Winnipeg from 1979 to 1992. He is presently Chancellor of the University of Manitoba and Honorary Consul-General of Japan for Manitoba. Norrie received his BA in 1950 from United College, and a law degree from the University of Manitoba in 1955. Among other honours, Norrie has had his bust in the Assiniboine Park Citizen's Hall of Fame cast by renowned Winnipeg sculptor Leo Mol.

1. **Getting downtown was easy**. There weren't too many cars and you could walk from most places in the city.

2. **Shopping downtown**. Eaton's and the Bay were thriving, and Eaton's Grill Room was a favorite place for Saturday lunch. The statue of Timothy Eaton on the main floor of Eaton's was also a favorite meeting place.

3. **Getting into the professions**. If you wanted to go to Law School or Medical School and could pass your undergraduate courses with a reasonable average, you had a good chance of getting into your chosen profession. Who ever heard of LSATs or MSATs?

4. **Having fun as you got educated**. In the 50s we spent as much (or more) time on extra-curricular activities as we did on studies. No need to be a semi-professional athlete to play on the basketball or volleyball team. We joined the Glee Club and performed in operettas, wrote for *The Manitoban* (the student newspaper) and served on the Student Council — all as volunteers and while carrying a full class load.

5. **Cheap transportation**. Buses (and streetcars) were cheap and few students had cars so taking the bus was normal. You met friends or made new ones on the bus and, since the city was smaller, got around easily.

RELIGIOUS AFFILIATION

Denomination	1991	2001
Roman Catholic	293,950	292,965
Protestant	533,945	475,185
Christian Orthodox	20,660	15,645
Christian other	16,175	44,535

The Winnipeg General Strike

At 11:00 am on May 15, 1919, between 25,000 and 30,000 Winnipeg workers walked off the job, launching Canada's most famous strike. The action brought the city of 175,000 to a standstill, as factories closed, streetcars came to a halt, and shops locked their doors.

Earlier that spring, metal and building trade unions had united to demand higher wages and recognition from their respective employers. After negotiations broke down, the unions obtained support from the Winnipeg Trade and Labour Council to engage in a general strike. Joining the factory, foundry and railway workers were firefighters, waterworks employees, postal workers and even the city police. A Central Strike Committee oversaw the conduct of the strike, and coordinated the delivery of essential services.

Shortly after the strike began, Winnipeg's most powerful manufacturers, politicians and bankers organized an opposition. With the support of the leading newspapers, the Citizens' Committee of 1,000 declared the strike a revolutionary conspiracy led by European agitators and Bolsheviks. They petitioned the federal government to intervene.

On May 22, 1919, two federal ministers arrived in Winnipeg for talks with the Citizens Committee, but refused to meet with the Strike Committee. Instead, the federal government passed legislation to broaden the criminal code definition of sedition, and amend

Jewish	13,670	13,035
Muslim	3,520	5,095
Buddhist	5,255	5,745
Hindu	3,470	3,840
Sikh	3,490	5,485

Source: Statistics Canada.

the immigration act so that British-born striking workers could more easily be deported. Subsequently, ten strike leaders were arrested.

Despite this intimidation, the strike, which had produced sympathy actions in other cities including Brandon, Calgary, Regina and Vancouver, continued. On June 21, thousands of strikers gathered in Winnipeg's old Market Square to protest the arrests. In response, the mayor called in the North West Mounted Police.

The crowds dispersed, only to be accosted by the city's replacement law enforcement officers, thugs equipped with baseball bats and wagon spokes. As the situation degenerated into chaos, the army patrolled the streets in vehicles mounted with machine guns. In the end, thirty people were injured and two people killed in what became known as "Bloody Saturday."

On June 26, cowed by government violence and intimidation, the remaining strike leaders declared an end to the strike. Any further action, they agreed, would be conducted at the political level, not on the streets.

After the strikers returned to work, the jailed organizers were released. These leaders included J.S. Woodsworth who would later go on to found Canada's first socialist political party, the Co-operative Commonwealth Federation (CCF), forerunner to the New Democratic Party (NDP). Although the striking workers returned to much the same conditions against which they had fought, their efforts served to inspire future generations of labour organizers.

THE GREAT DEPRESSION

Manitoba's rapidly developing economy foundered when the Great Depression hit in 1929. Low grain prices coupled with recurrent drought and crop failure devastated the province. In 1932, commodity prices plummeted, not because of climatic conditions, but due to oversupply in the world market.

Farm income in Manitoba was cut by 80 percent, and farmers were ruined by the high debt loads they had incurred expanding and mechanizing during more prosperous times. At the same time, drought hit the prairies. Fierce hot winds created dust storms and nothing would grow. There were a couple of years of respite from the heat, but they were followed by scorching temperatures and the longest, hottest summers on record. Millions of acres of Manitoba topsoil simply blew away.

By 1937 lakes had gone dry, locusts swarmed the prairies, and farmers were cutting Canada thistle to feed their starving animals. Short on food, some families resorted to eating gophers. In a few short years, Manitoba had gone from a booming province that beckoned newcomers, to one of the most impoverished regions of the country. In response, social welfare programs were established by the provincial and municipal governments, and locals pooled their resources by establishing credit unions and cooperatives.

With the outbreak of World War II, the rains returned, as did job opportunities and economic growth.

Did you know...

that Manitoba has the largest population of people of Icelandic origin outside of Iceland? The New Iceland Heritage Museum in Gimli celebrates the history of the Icelandic, people as well as the substantial immigration to Manitoba that occurred in the 1870s and 1880s.

AN ELECTRIFYING STORY

Today, Manitoba is renowned for its hydro-electric infrastructure and boasts a total of 14 generating stations on the Nelson, Winnipeg, Saskatchewan and Laurie rivers. Over the years, the public utility, Manitoba Hydro, has grown into a veritable North American power-house, providing electricity not only to Manitobans, but also to com-

Take 5 DANNY SCHUR'S FIVE REASONS
THE WINNIPEG GENERAL STRIKE STILL MATTERS

Danny Schur is the composer/producer and co-author (with Rick Chafe) of the award-winning musical *Strike!* set during the 1919 Winnipeg General Strike — Canada's most famous labour uprising.

1. **The strike (as a historical event or musical) is a metaphor for a society in which civic order breaks down.** The lessons of compromise and tolerance learned in Winnipeg in 1919 can be applied to any contemporary international conflict.

2. **The legacy of the 1919 strike continues to inspire labour, and historians, nationally and internationally.** Witness the CBC production of "Bloody Saturday" — a nationally broadcast television special in June, 2007.

3. **Warts and all, the strike is unique to Winnipeg.** The particular mix of ethnicities that comprised labour combined with a combustible class of war veterans and led to the bloody culmination of the strike. Nowhere in the world did a general strike last so long, divide so bitterly, nor inspire so lengthy, and controversial, a legacy.

4. **The circumstances that lead to the 1919 strike read like the headlines of today:** economic downturn on the heels of war and pandemic, societal paranoia over terrorism, and widespread discrimination towards immigrants.

5. **The Canadian Museum for Human Rights will be located in Winnipeg** — the city that spawned not only the 1919 strike, but also Canada's female suffrage movement.

munities in neighbouring provinces and a number of US states.

The first electric light in Manitoba was turned on in Winnipeg on March 12, 1873 by the Honourable Robert A. Davis, owner of Davis House, a hotel on Main Street. In 1880, Manitoba Electric & Gas Lighting Company was incorporated, and it was followed by a number of other purveyors of heat and light. Still very little of Manitoba's electricity went for residential use. Most electricity in the late 19th century was produced by steam plants and was used for lighting streets and businesses, as well as powering Winnipeg's streetcars.

In 1900, the Minnedosa River Plant became the first hydro-electric generating station in Manitoba. This new technology was the key to eventually providing electricity to every household in the province. Rural electrification became a reality in 1921 when service was extended to the towns of Carman, Minnedosa, Morden, Roland and Virden by Manitoba Power, a publically-owned company that had been incorporated the previous year.

Following WWII, the provincial government launched a Farm Electrification program. In addition to making domestic life much more comfortable, electricity greatly increased farm productivity. Hen house lighting lengthened winter days, allowing flocks to eat more and lay more eggs. Electric pumps helped keep water running for livestock, and electric motors powered threshing and grain handling machinery. Nearly 1,000 farms were connected the first year, with electricity spreading to all of southern Manitoba in the next decade.

In 1961, the provincial government consolidated all electrical utilities in one Crown Corporation via the Manitoba Hydro Act. That same year, northern areas, including many remote First Nations communities, were connected to the provincial power system; until then they had relied on diesel generators for power.

Today, the province is exploring new ways to generate electricity. In 2005, Manitoba's first wind turbines were erected in St. Leon, and there are plans for more. Manitoba Hydro now counts 517,000 electricity customers and 260,000 gas customers.

They Said It

> Hudson Bay is certainly a country that Sinbad the Sailor never saw, as he makes no mention of mosquitoes.
>
> **– Explorer and Hudson's Bay Company man David Thompson, a resident at Fort Prince of Wales (now Churchill) from 1784 to 1812.**

EDUCATION

For decades, the one-room school house was a fixture on the Manitoba landscape. One of the first schools was established in 1829 by two Métis sisters, Angelique and Marguerite Nolan, and provided education to Catholic girls.

In fact, when Manitoba became a province, it was with provisions for a publically-funded dual school system for English Protestants and French Catholics. That system was abolished 20 years later when the provincial government established English-only public schools. Catholics and French speakers were bitterly opposed to the measure, and the long running controversy came to be known as the "Manitoba Schools Question."

It wasn't until the 1960s, when Duff Roblin was premier, that all one-room schools were consolidated, and French language public education reinstituted, although in a limited way. Francophones regained full control of a publically-funded school system only in the 1990s.

Did you know...

that Manitoba's Clifford Sifton, who served as Liberal Minister of the Interior under Wilfred Laurier from 1896 to 1905, was not only responsible for policies which brought thousands to the Canadian west, he was also one of the first owners of the *Manitoba Free Press*, (precursor of today's *Winnipeg Free Press*)?

They Said It

THE MEDIUM IS THE MESSAGE

Manitoba has a rich communications and media history. It's not surprising that modern media's most famous guru, Marshall McLuhan, spent his formative years in the province and received Bachelor's and Master's degrees from the University of Manitoba.

The first newspaper on the Canadian prairies was the *Nor'Wester*, founded in the Red River Settlement by William Buckingham and William Coldwell. The inaugural issue appeared on December 28, 1859 and publication continued until the offices were seized by Louis Riel in 1869.

Three years later, the *Manitoba Free Press* appeared on the scene, eventually morphing into the *Winnipeg Free Press*, thanks to the overwhelming concentration of the province's population in its capital city. A competitor in the form of the *Winnipeg Tribune* soon arose, publishing for 90 years until it folded in 1980. The "Trib," as it was affectionately known, was quickly replaced by the *Winnipeg Sun*, a tabloid heavy on sports and crime that locals say is much easier to read on the bus!

Did you know...

that WWII master spy Sir William Stephenson was born and raised in Winnipeg? Stephenson, who was also a WWI fighter pilot, wrote the book *A Man Called Intrepid* and was portrayed by David Niven in the 1979 miniseries of the same name.

Print is far from the only medium to enjoy a vibrant life in Manitoba. The province is the home of CanWest Global, the media empire founded by local magnate Israel (Izzy) Asper. In addition to a number of newspapers, CanWest owns radio and television stations, Internet portals and the naming rights, in one form or another, to a half dozen prominent buildings in Winnipeg.

Take 5 FIVE WINNIPEG STREET NAMES
AND THEIR ORIGINS

1. **Broadway** (1873). The city's largest boulevard, it was named by the Hudson's Bay Company as the primary east-west artery through Winnipeg. Several towns in Manitoba have thoroughfares with the same stand-alone name (no designation such as street or avenue is attached).

2. **Pembina Highway** (1908). Pembina is the trail leading to Fort Pembina and North Dakota, just as Portage Avenue was the trail leading to Portage la Prairie.

3. **Annabelle Street** (c.1910). Famous for its brothels, this street in Winnipeg's Point Douglas neighborhood was named after one of its most illustrious madams. The red light district has since moved to Albert Street, named after Queen Victoria's consort.

4. **Valour Road** (1945). Formerly Pine Street, it was renamed to honour three men — Robert Shankland, Leo Clarks, and Fred Hall — who lived on the street before going on to win the Victoria Cross for bravery during World War II.

5. **Lagimodiere Boulevard** (1971). Commonly called "Ladge" by locals, this rapid road heading north to cottage country was named after Jean Baptiste Lagimodière. He and his wife Marie-Anne Gaboury were the first white couple to settle the area. They were also the grandparents of Louis Riel.

HUNGRY?

Manitobans have come a long way from Pemmican in a pouch and bannock cooked over an open fire. Waves of immigration have brought such staples as Ukrainian perogies and Mennonite farmer's sausage to local tables.

Lately, there's been a growing interest in home grown foods, and locally-produced food and drink. Wild rice and pickerel can be found on the menu at almost any reputable Manitoba restaurant. The former is a grain harvested wild from Manitoba's wetlands, and the latter a mild-tasting fish, also called walleye, found mainly in Lake Winnipeg. Ice houses on the lake kept the fish fresh in the early days, but now they're available in the fridge and freezer of any good grocery store.

ALL THE LIVE LONG DAY

The arrival of the railway transformed Manitoba into a transportation hub and the gateway between east and west. Trains were essential in transporting grain from the prairies to eastern ports, and immigrants from the east to the prairies.

From the 1870s to the 1920s, Northern Pacific and Manitoba Railway Company, the Canadian Northern, the Grand Trunk Pacific Railroad (later CPR) and the Canadian National Railway all built yards in Winnipeg at the forks of the Red and Assiniboine Rivers.

The first locomotive arrived in St. Boniface in 1877, five years before the Canadian Pacific Railway (CPR) signed a contract to build a transcontinental railway. Thanks to pressure from Manitobans, the

Did you know...

that from the early 1900s to the 1950s, trains brought revelers to the resort towns of Grand Beach and Victoria Beach on the east side of Lake Winnipeg? During the Roaring Twenties, 50 cents bought a round trip and a night of dancing at the bandstand in Grand Beach.

Take 5 FIVE THINGS
MADE IN MANITOBA

1. The Harlequin Romance publishing empire was founded in Winnipeg in 1949.
2. The Rh immunoglobulin, a vaccine which prevents a deadly blood disorder in newborns, was developed by Drs. Chown and Bowman at Manitoba's Rh Institute in 1968.
3. Dr. Baldur Stefansson of the University of Manitoba developed hybrid canola seeds in 1974. The breakthrough proved key in canola's boom as an agricultural product.
4. Winnipeg pioneered the 911 emergency telephone number system. Originally using the numbers 999, the program was launched in 1959 at the behest of Mayor Stephen Juba.
5. The international polling company Angus Reid Group was established in Winnipeg in 1979.

CPR agreed to build the tracks through Winnipeg, rather than Selkirk as previously planned. This move confirmed Winnipeg as the province's commercial capital, resulting in an economic explosion that drew many to the city.

Today, the railway still employs thousands of Manitobans, although the system now primarily moves freight rather than people. One exception is the train to Churchill, a popular mode of transportation for tourists from all over the world who come to see the area's renowned polar bears.

Did you know...

that the Alpine Club of Canada was founded in Winnipeg in 1906? Now based in Canmore, AB, the Alpine Club is Canada's national mountaineering organization.

GOING MOBILE

Ever since Professor J. Kenrick turned the crank on the province's first motor car in 1901, automobiles have continued to multiply on Manitoba streets and highways. In fact, in 2006 there were 923,732 registered motor vehicles — almost enough for every man, woman, child and newborn to get behind the wheel!

Pavement, on the other hand, has not quite kept pace. Despite the fact that the first strip of pavement was laid seven years before the arrival of the first car, Manitoba is better known for its potholes than its asphalt. Could it have something to do with those large snowplows that scrape the roads every winter?

HOLD THE LINE

In 1878, Horace McDougall strung a wire between his Winnipeg house and the telegraph office next door where he worked. The telephone had come to Manitoba. McDougall soon became an agent for Bell, selling the new gadget to whoever could afford the steep $60 yearly fee. Within a few months, the Custom House, the Manitoba Free Press and the railway station were connected by phone.

Residential use, however, was rare in the early days; in 1881 Winnipeg counted only 26 subscribers. Telephones were both expensive and awkward. Often referred to as "butter stamps," one receiver was employed for both talking and listening. Users switched from mouth to ear, tapping on the mouthpiece to attract the other party's attention. Moreover, telephones worked only in pairs. To address the problem, the city set up a switchboard and hired its first telephone operators. Teenage boys had traditionally been employed in the telegraph business, and seemed naturals for the burgeoning telephone industry; however, their frequent pranks and tendency to chat with young female callers resulted in their replacement by women.

As there were no phone numbers in the early days, operators had to know all subscribers in the city by name. The first phone directory was produced in 1881 with a list of 42 people. By the following year, usage had grown to 235 telephones on 70 miles of wire. The province of Manitoba realized that this new technology would need managing, and purchased the telephone system from Bell for $3.3 million in 1905. In 1908, Manitoba Government Telephones became the first public telephone utility in North America.

By 1962, the number of telephones in the province had reached 300,000 and the public utility rebranded itself Manitoba Telephone Services. Now known to Manitobans simply as MTS, the company maintains a high profile with its popular bison advertising campaign, and its sponsorship of Winnipeg Olympic skating medalist Cindy Klassen.

PUBLIC TRANSPORTATION

The first attempt to bring public transit to Manitoba ended dismally. In 1877 the North-West Angle Stage folded after one day due to a lack of passengers and mud that was too deep for its horse-drawn vehicles to navigate. The Winnipeg Street Railway Company, also horse powered, took up the challenge and proved successful.

A happy day for horses occurred in 1892, when Manitoba's first electric streetcar debuted in Winnipeg. In 1913, Brandon's system was similarly electrified. By that time, the air above Winnipeg's rail embedded streets was a web of electrical wires and there was an extensive streetcar network. In the 1920s, gas-powered buses started to appear as a solution for inter-urban transport, and also began to make headway within the city of Winnipeg.

Winnipeg's public transit system was transferred to public ownership in 1950. At that time, electric streetcars were gradually being replaced by trolleys; the final streetcar ride was on September 19, 1955. Trolleys continued to operate until 1970 when the city of Winnipeg's Transit System switched the fleet entirely to buses. Today, there are no signs that streetcars ever roamed the streets of Manitoba's cities.

Public transit ridership has declined sharply in the last several decades, and the dominant current mode of transportation in

Manitoba is far and away the private automobile. In 1982, Winnipeg Transit recorded 60 million passenger trips, but by 2007 this figure had fallen to 41.2 million.

The good news is that recent figures represent an increase from the 37.7 million rides recorded in 2003, and high gas prices are further augmenting ridership. Discussions for implementing a rapid mass transit system have been on-going for decades, but with little result.

Adult transit fare

1957	$0.15
1969	$0.25
1982	$0.60
1990	$1.10
2002	$1.75
2008	$2.25

DOWNHILL ALL THE WAY

At first glance, alpine skiing and the flat prairies of Manitoba would seem to be as incompatible as deep sea fishing in Alberta. Yet, in the 1940s, the province counted more than 5,000 active skiers, with upwards of 1,000 enthusiasts taking the ski trains down to resorts such as La Riviere and Snow Valley every weekend.

By 1960, there were no less than 15 ski hills/resorts in the province and nary a cross-country ski to be seen. In fact, it was not until the 1970s that the Nordic version of the sport became popular. Until then, it was downhill all the way.

So where are all these Manitoba mountains where people go to ski? In most cases, the hills are actually valleys carved out by rivers. Today, the province has eight ski resorts, including the popular Asessippi Ski Area, a 25-run winter village near the Saskatchewan border that boasts a vertical drop of 152 m.

Weblinks

Manitobia

www.manitobia.ca/cocoon/launch/en/themesSelectionPage

Manitobia is produced by the Manitoba Library Consortium and partners including universities and government archives and provides a
wealth of historical information spanning the period from Manitoba's
birth to the strike of 1919. Arranged thematically, the site includes
photos, biographies, maps, timelines and all of the provinces' newspapers, with access to actual published pages.

Manitoba Historical Society

www.mhs.mb.ca

Equipped with a powerful search engine to hone in on specific topics,
this web site features colourful articles about every period in
Manitoba's history. Certainly not a grab-and-go option, it is a great
resource for those who have the time to read.

Manitoba Archives

www.gov.mb.ca/chc/archives/index.html

For the true history or genealogy buff, this site offers access to the ultimate collection of primary materials. It is also home to the Hudson's
Bay Company Archives.

The Winnipeg Time Machine

www.siamandas.com/time_machine/

Award-winning photographer and film maker George Siamandas brings
together more than 250 stories of Winnipeg and Manitoba history that
he has presented on CBC's Information Radio over two decades.

The First People

IN THE BEGINNING

For over 6,000 years, a number of Manitoba's First Nations have been meeting at a place well known to contemporary Winnipeggers — The Forks, which represents the confluence of the Red and Assiniboine Rivers. The rivers provided Manitoba's First Nations with a transportation thoroughfare, as well as fish to eat, and water to drink and nourish crops.

The story of Manitoba's First Peoples is one of perseverance and resistance: the struggle to survive in an isolated area beset by a harsh climate, and, equally, the battle against colonization, and the expropriation of traditionally held lands by explorers and settlers of European origin.

Manitoba's First Peoples are found throughout the province, on rural reserves and in small towns, as well as in the city of Winnipeg. Their story is still being written as Manitoba's sizeable and vibrant Aboriginal community grapples with both challenges and opportunities unimaginable to their forefathers.

FIRST ENCOUNTER

The first encounters the Aboriginal residents of Manitoba had with the white man is thought to have been in 1668, when the *Nonsuch* — a ship commissioned by the government of England — arrived on the shores of Hudson Bay to establish a post and develop the fur trade in Manitoba. The Hudson's Bay Company (HBC) was officially founded in 1670, and the territory of Rupert's Land was established. Over subsequent years, HBC bought many furs from the First Nations people it encountered. As the company expanded its operations, not just trade but the active colonization and displacement of Manitoba's first residents occurred.

LANGUAGES

There are six major languages spoken by the Aboriginal peoples of Manitoba. One of the most prolific groups speaks Ojibway (which is also known as Anishnawbe or Saulteaux), a language common to First Nations who settled around Lake Winnipeg. Cree is the primary language spoken by First Nations of central Manitoba. Oji-Cree, a combination of Ojibway and Cree, is primarily spoken in northeastern Manitoba around Hudson Bay and Island Lake. Both Ojibway and

Did you know...

that Pemmican Publications is a Winnipeg-based publisher of Métis literature? Founded in 1980, Pemmican's mandate is to promote Canadian Métis writers and illustrators through stories that capture and illuminate the Métis experience.

Did you know...

that the Métis Nation has its own flag? The flag is called the Métis Infinity Flag and is blue with a white infinity sign (similar to a figure 8.) It is the official flag of Louis Riel Day. The flag has represented the Métis since 1816, and symbolizes the joining of two cultures.

Cree are derived from the Algonquian linguistic family.

Aboriginals residing in southwestern Manitoba primarily speak the Dakota language — a derivative of the Siouan linguistic family. Dene (also known as Chipewyan) is spoken in the far north at Tadoule Lake and Lac Brochet, and is derived from the Athapaskan linguistic family. Some Métis speak Michif (also spelled Mitchif,) a unique blend of French and Cree.

Sources: The Encyclopedia of Manitoba, "500 Nations" and "Native Languages" websites.

Take 5 PHIL FONTAINE'S FIVE
FAVOURITE MANITOBA PLACES

Now Ottawa-based as National Chief of the Assembly of First Nations, Phil Fontaine gets to visit lots of great places. But he still has a big spot in his heart for Manitoba, the province where he grew up as the youngest son in a large Ojibway family on the Sagkeeng First Nation. After Fontaine's father died when he was six, he spent large portions of the following 10 years living at an Indian Residential School. Fontaine remembers the hardships and abuse he endured at the school, but also the love and strength that his mother (the first Indian woman in Canada elected to an Indian band council) demonstrated in raising her 12 children after the unexpected death of her husband.

1. **Lone Island**. I love the wild rice fields here. One of my earliest memories is going to pick wild rice with my family and then eating it for dinner.
2. **Island Lake**. This is a very beautiful place where you can see many islands. I have fond memories of going fishing from St. Therese Point with my friends.
3. **The Forks**. This is the point where early trading took place between indigenous people and Europeans. It has historical significance to First Nations, Manitobans, and all Canadians.
4. **St. Boniface**. I find this to be a very spiritual place. It gives me a serene feeling because of its very old buildings and richness in history.
5. **The Mouth of the Winnipeg River at Traverse Bay**. I have fond memories of taking my young family there. We loved gathering wild berries. We would also watch the waves crashing on the shore for hours. It was very calming.

They Said It

TREATIES

The First Peoples of the area now known as Manitoba signed a number of treaties, transferring land ownership from the Dene, Ojibway, Cree and Oji-Cree to the federal government of Canada. Treaties 1, 2, 3, 4 and 5 were signed between 1871 and 1875 with some later amendments. Treaty 10 was signed in 1907.

Not all Aboriginal groups in the province were asked to sign treaties with the government. For example, the Dakota had no treaty with the Canadian government as they were considered "American Indians" because much of their tribe lived in the US.

Unlike many of their First Nations brothers and sisters, the Métis did not sign historic treaties and did not have special standing, despite land grants stemming from the 1870 Manitoba Act. In the years following the Act, large numbers of Métis left the area (which was becoming increasingly inhospitable to them), surrendering their claim

Did you know...

that Winnipeg Blue Bombers kicker Troy Westwood, who records under the pseudonym "Little Hawk," was nominated for a 2008 Juno in the Aboriginal Recording of the Year category, even though he is not of Aboriginal descent?

to the land in the process.

In recent decades, the Manitoba Métis have reorganized and resumed their efforts to achieve recognition as a nation. In 1981, a massive land claim lawsuit was filed against the federal and provincial governments to reestablish the rights to 566,000 hectares of land along the Red and Assiniboine rivers that the Métis contend belongs to them. The case was dismissed in 2007 and is currently under appeal.

Sources: The Encyclopedia of Manitoba and the Manitoba Métis Federation.

Take 5 FIVE PLACES TO LEARN ABOUT
MANITOBA'S FIRST NATIONS

1. **The Forks**, Winnipeg. The confluence of the Red and Assiniboine rivers has been a meeting place for Manitobans for over 6,000 years. The "Oodena Celebration Circle," "Wall Through Time" and "Assiniboine River Walk" provide information detailing Aboriginal life on the rivers and surrounding area.

2. **Circle of Life Thunderbird House**, Winnipeg. A contemporary building that echoes traditional First Nations' structures, Thunderbird House is a meeting place for Winnipeg's First Nations community and offers workshops, concerts, and interpretative programs.

3. **Kenosewun Visitor Centre and Museum**, Lockport (about 30 km northeast of Winnipeg). The Kenosewun Centre features a small museum devoted to Aboriginal artifacts and the lives of First Nations people in the area. Kenosewun is a rich hunting, fishing and agricultural site on the Red River whose name in Cree means "place of many fish."

4. **Riding Mountain National Park**, near Dauphin in southwestern Manitoba. The 3,000 km^2 park has been home to Aboriginal peoples (including the Keeseekoowenin Ojibway First Nations who still inhabit the area) for 6,000 years. Plentiful water, boreal forest, aspen, and grasses made the area a popular hunting and fishing grounds.

5. **Eskimo Museum**, Churchill. The art, tools and culture of the Inuit people.

Bio CHIEF PEGUIS

The great chief was an abandoned baby, found on a pile of woodchips by an elderly woman who nicknamed him, "Peeh-qua-is" meaning "Little Chip" in their Saulteaux (Ojibway) language. He later changed his name to Peguis, meaning "Woodchip."

Born in 1774 in the Great Lakes area near Sault Ste. Marie, Ontario, Peguis came to Manitoba in the late 1790s with the fur trade and made his home along the Red River, where he died in 1864. Chief Peguis was a friend to the white settlers and the Hudson's Bay Company. He welcomed Lord Selkirk and his Red River newcomers who came to the Netley Creek area along the Red River in 1812. He showed the settlers how to hunt and how to live off the land.

Peguis was one of five chiefs who signed an 1817 treaty with Lord Selkirk specifying land for settlers in exchange for annual tobacco payments. This was the first land treaty signed in western Canada.

Peguis was described as a small, solid man with a strong voice and a nose that had been partly bitten off during a tribal dispute. This spawned the nickname, "Cut-Nosed Chief" by the white settlers. Peguis was baptized late in life by the Anglican Church (an act which required him to give up three of his four wives) and took the name William King.

Despite his apparent embrace of the Europeans, a few years before his death, Peguis became dissatisfied with the occupation of large amounts of territory not included in the 1817 treaty, and also questioned whether the treaty lands had been permanently surrendered as claimed the Europeans. The matter was not resolved until 1871 when the federal government negotiated a treaty with Peguis's son, seven years after the chief's death.

The largest First Nation in Manitoba is the Peguis First Nation — named in honour of Chief Peguis. Winnipeg also has a school named after the chief: Chief Peguis Junior High School, located in the River East Transcona School Division.

POPULATION

Manitoba's past, present and future are highly influenced by its First Nations, as people of Aboriginal descent make up more than 15 percent of the province's total population today. The Aboriginal demographic represents the fastest growing segment of Manitoba's population. Gauging the precise number of Manitoba Aboriginals is difficult, however, as Manitoba's large Métis community has historically not been fully counted as a component of the Native population.

- Number of people of self-declared Aboriginal descent: 175,395
- Number who are of North American First Nations heritage: 100,640

Manito Ahbee:
A Festival For All Nations

Manitoba has a rich, diverse and thriving Aboriginal culture that produces a tremendous assortment of First Nations and Métis artists, musicians, authors and other cultural contributors. So it was only natural to develop a venue that would bring them all together, and in 2006 the Manito Ahbee Festival was born.

Billed as "A Festival for All Nations," Manito Ahbee is held yearly in Winnipeg over a 10-day span in late October and early November. It is an Aboriginal peoples' event that combines music, visual art, theatre, and dance, along with an International Pow Wow competition, an Aboriginal youth summit, and a marketplace and trade show.

The name "Manito Ahbee" means "where the Creator sits," and refers to a traditional gathering spot for First Nations located in Whiteshell Provincial Park. Festival activities, which are open to all, take place at the MTS Centre, the Winnipeg Convention Centre and a number of other smaller venues.

Winnipeg has hosted the Aboriginal Peoples Choice Music Awards since their inception in 2006. The awards (shaped in the form of a feather) are presented at Manito Ahbee, and honour the best in Aboriginal music from across Canada and the US.

- Number who are counted as members of the Métis Nation: 71,805
- Number who are Inuit: 565
- Percentage of Aboriginals who live in Winnipeg: 36.3

The Métis

Manitoba is considered the birthplace of the Métis Nation. The word Métis means "mixed," and describes a people whose ancestry dates to the late 18th century, when Europeans came to Manitoba to develop the fur trade. They inter-married with local Aboriginals, and the result was a people of mixed blood called the Métis. The Métis are certainly not limited to Manitoba, as people of the Métis Nation reside in most Canadian provinces, as well as several US states.

The Métis National Council says that a Métis is defined as a person who self-identifies as a Métis, and is of historic Métis Nation ancestry – a status quite distinct from other Aboriginal peoples. The Métis have had to fight hard to find their place in society. They were known as "half-breeds" for much of the 20th century, and fell between the cracks as they were not "white," yet did not receive the benefits of full-blood treaty Indians.

Louis Riel is Canada's best-known Métis, and defended the rights of his people in Manitoba and Saskatchewan with almost messianic zeal. Over time, Riel has become a Manitoba hero – many refer to him as the "father" or "founder" of Manitoba, and he is the namesake of Louis Riel Day, the Manitoba holiday first celebrated on February 19, 2008.

Today, most Manitoba Métis live in the city of Winnipeg, although there is also a sizeable community in St. Laurent, which is located about 80 kilometres north of Winnipeg near the southeastern shores of Lake Manitoba. The rural setting allows for a lifestyle focused on hunting, trapping and fishing, enabling Métis traditions to remain alive. This maintenance of traditional ways attracted the attention of the Smithsonian Institute, which visited St. Laurent in 2004 and established their Métis exhibit based on what they saw. The town's most famous son is Yvon Dumont, Former Lieutenant Governor of Manitoba.

Take 5 FIVE FACTS ABOUT THE
ABORIGINAL PEOPLES TELEVISION NETWORK (APTN)

1. The APTN was officially launched in Winnipeg on September 1, 1999 and now has 11 news bureaus across the country.
2. APTN has a total of 120 employees throughout Canada, more than 75 percent of whom are of Aboriginal descent.
3. APTN broadcasts approximately 56 percent of its programming in English, 16 percent in French and 28 percent in a variety of Aboriginal languages including Inuktitut, Cree, Inuinaqtuun, Ojibway, Inuvialuktun, Mohawk, Dene, Gwich'in, Miqma'aq, Slavey, Dogrib, Chipweyan, Tlingit and Michif.
4. In its short history, APTN has won numerous awards including nine Geminis and several Canadian Association of Broadcasters awards.
5. On March 3, 2008, APTN began broadcasting in high definition.
Source: APTN.

- Percentage of Native American First Nations who live in Winnipeg; 24.8
- Percentage of Manitoba Métis who live in Winnipeg: 52.1

Source: Statistics Canada and Manitoba Bureau of Statistics.

They Said It

"*My people will sleep for 100 years, and when they awake, it will be the artists who give them back their spirit.*"

– Louis Riel

Did you know...

that actor Adam Beach, a member of the Saulteaux First Nation, was born in 1972 in Ashern on the Dog Creek Indian Reserve? Beach has appeared in numerous television shows including Law & Order: Special Victims Unit, as well as starring in movies such as Squanto: A Warrior's Tale, Smoke Signals and Windtalkers.

RESERVES

Manitoba has 66 First Nations (this is what people of Aboriginal descent generally prefer to call themselves) or Indian Bands (a term devised by the federal government to differentiate First Nations), each with its own treaty or tract of land that is administered in cooperation with the federal government. However, there are 200 reserves in the province, as several of the large bands have more than one reserve to accommodate their

 TINA KEEPER

ACTRESS TURNED POLITICIAN

Tina Keeper was born in 1962 in the tiny northern Manitoba community of Norway House, and spent her early years on the Chemawawin Cree Nation before moving to Winnipeg. She is a member of the Norway House Cree Nation. That's a long way from Ottawa, where Keeper has been residing since being elected Liberal Member of Parliament for the Churchill Region in January 2006.

While in Ottawa, Tina has been instrumental in getting Aboriginal issues brought to the forefront. She is currently the Liberal Party's Special Advisor for Aboriginal Outreach, and is a Member of Parliament's Standing Committee on Aboriginal Affairs and Northern Development. She has also served as the Official Opposition's Health Critic and Heritage Critic.

Tina Keeper's move onto the political stage is hardly surprising, given her background. Her father, Joseph Irvine Keeper, was a founding member of the National Indian Council, and has been inducted into the Order of Canada, and her mother, Phyllis Keeper, is an Anglican priest.

Keeper has an unusual combination of honours; she has received an Aboriginal Achievement Award, is a member of the Order of Manitoba, and won a Gemini Award. Keeper received the Gemini for her portrayal of a police constable in the popular television CBC series, *North of 60*, which ran from 1992 to 1998.

Keeper has offices in Ottawa, Thompson and Sagkeeng, and when not busy with politics, continues to work in television; she has written, directed and produced more than a dozen segments of "Sharing Circle," an Aboriginal documentary television series.